EVERYTHING.

Series

Dear Reader,

Danke schön! Thanks for choosing *The Everything®
German Phrase Book* as your vehicle for learning or
brushing up on your German. I think you're going
to find it easy to use and the perfect companion for
your journey through the German-speaking world.

My long-held interest in German is no mystery.
Some in my family came from Germany, so I had the
advantage of hearing the language from childhood.
When I began my formal study of German, I real-
ized my interest in it was the fundamental part of my
future profession, and I ended up in graduate school
in Hamburg. That marvelous city became my second
home and my base for adventures into other areas of
Germany. After I became a teacher of German in the
United States, I never lost the need to travel back to
my second home and became acquainted with every
region of Germany, Austria, and Switzerland.

My hope is that this book will help to guide you in
discovering the wonderful things and friendly people that the German-speaking countries of Europe
have to offer. You're going to be surprised how many
smiles you'll earn when you approach a shopkeeper
or passerby with one of your German phrases.

Have fun learning. Viel Spaß!

Edward Swick

The EVERYTHING® Series

These handy, accessible books give you all you need to tackle a difficult project, gain a new hobby, or even brush up on something you learned back in school but have since forgotten. You can read from cover to cover or just pick out information from our four useful boxes.

E **Alerts:** Urgent warnings

E **Essentials:** Quick handy tips

E **Facts:** Important snippets of information

E **Questions:** Answers to common questions

When you're done reading, you can finally say you know **EVERYTHING®**!

PUBLISHER Karen Cooper

DIRECTOR OF ACQUISITIONS AND INNOVATION Paula Munier

MANAGING EDITOR, EVERYTHING SERIES Lisa Laing

COPY CHIEF Casey Ebert

ACQUISITIONS EDITOR Lisa Laing

ASSOCIATE DEVELOPMENT EDITOR Elizabeth Kassab

EDITORIAL ASSISTANT Hillary Thompson

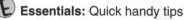

Visit the entire Everything® series at *www.everything.com*

THE
EVERYTHING®
GERMAN
PHRASE
BOOK

A quick refresher for any situation

Edward Swick, M.A.

Avon, Massachusetts

An Everything® Series Book.
Everything® and everything.com® are registered
trademarks of F+W Media, Inc.

Published by Adams Media, an F+W Media Company
57 Littlefield Street, Avon, MA 02322 U.S.A.
www.adamsmedia.com

ISBN 10: 1-59869-755-2
ISBN 13: 978-1-59869-755-1

Printed in Canada.

J I H G F E D C B A

Library of Congress Cataloging-in-Publication Data
is available from the publisher.

This publication is designed to provide accurate and authoritative information with regard to the subject matter covered. It is sold with the understanding that the publisher is not engaged in rendering legal, accounting, or other
professional advice. If legal advice or other expert assistance is required, the
services of a competent professional person should be sought.
—From a *Declaration of Principles* jointly adopted by a Committee of the
American Bar Association and a Committee of Publishers and Associations

Many of the designations used by manufacturers and sellers to distinguish
their products are claimed as trademarks. Where those designations appear
in this book and Adams Media was aware of a trademark claim, the designations have been printed with initial capital letters.

This book is available at quantity discounts for bulk purchases.
For information, please call 1-800-289-0963.

Visit the entire *Everything*® series at *www.everything.com*

Contents

The Top Ten German Phrases
You Should Know

1. Do you speak English? *Sprechen Sie Englisch?* (SHPREHCH en zee ENG lish)

2. Hello. *Guten Tag.* (GOO ten tuck)

3. Goodbye. *Auf Wiedersehen.* (owf VEE duh zay en)

4. My name is . . . *Ich heiße* . . . (eech HICE eh)

5. Where is . . . ? *Wo ist* . . . ? (voe ist)

6. How much does it cost? *Wie viel kostet es?* (vee feel KAWS tet ess)

7. I have . . . *Ich habe* . . . (eech HAH beh)

8. I don't have any . . . *Ich habe kein* . . . (eech HAH beh kine)

9. I need . . . *Ich brauche* . . . (eech BROWCH eh)

10. I would like . . . *Ich möchte* . . . (eech MERCH teh)

Introduction

It's never too late to learn a new language. But there is one prerequisite, which apparently you have, because you're reading this book: You need interest in the subject! Only you know exactly why you're interested in German. Perhaps a relative came from Germany years ago and you want to visit the site of your family's origins. Or maybe you just want to travel for fun or business and be able to communicate with the natives. It doesn't really matter what your reason is. What matters is that you have the interest, and that's the initial key to success.

Being able to communicate in German will open doors for you that most non-German-speaking travelers never even know exist. You can experience the native culture because culture and language are interrelated. Knowing what the street signs and advertisements mean, being able to read the headlines of a newspaper, understanding what the butcher is recommending to the customer next to you—these are things that only a German-speaking traveler can do. And *The Everything® German*

Phrase Book can provide you with the phrases and vocabulary that will give you the basic skills to do just that.

Naturally, just carrying this book around with you won't do the trick. You have to study the phrases and practice them. And remember that language—whether German, English, Russian, or Japanese—is first and foremost a spoken entity. You have to speak. You have to practice your phrases out loud. Just thinking them or reading them to yourself won't do. Languages are spoken.

German is used in other countries besides Germany. It is the official language of Austria, and it is a primary language of Switzerland and Liechtenstein. It certainly is no surprise that there are large German-speaking communities in the United States and Canada. Immigration from the German-speaking world in the last two centuries occurred on a large scale, so many North Americans speak or understand German. Since German is used in different regions, there are regional differences of pronunciation and vocabulary usage. For example, in English, someone in the south of the United States might say "skillet" while someone in the north might use the phrase "frying pan." In some English-speaking regions, you say "I'll wait for you." In other regions, you say, "I'll wait on you." Variations like this also occur in the German language. However, there is a standard German language that is generally accepted in all German-speaking regions, and that is the language used in *The Everything® German Phrase Book*.

Recently, the experts on the German language revised the rules for German spelling. Don't worry. That won't cause you a problem, because German spelling is for the most part phonetic. What the experts did was standardize a few letter combinations that differed depending upon the region in which they were used and depending upon the generation of the person who used them. For example, the German letter ß is sometimes replaced by *ss*, because they have the same pronunciation. But some people preferred ß and others preferred *ss*. So now there's a rule: If the vowel sound that precedes these letters is long, use ß. If it's short, use *ss*. Therefore, the word *weiß* (vice [white]) is spelled with ß, because the vowel is long. The word *dass* (duss [that]) is spelled with *ss*, because the vowel is short.

The three main sections of *The Everything*® *German Phrase Book* are the lessons, the phrases, and the appendices. Naturally, you should start with the lessons, which provide you with the basics of grammar and pronunciation as well as practical phrases. Chapter 1 introduces you to the German language and how it is both similar to and different from English. Chapter 2 provides you with the fundamentals of German grammar and structure. With a careful reading of these two chapters, you will have a basic understanding of German that will help to guide you through the other chapters.

Chapters 3 through 14 provide you with practical German phrases for a variety of situations. Each phrase is accompanied by its English equivalent translation (not all phrases can be translated word for word) and by the approximate English pronunciation of the German phrase. When there is no equivalent English pronunciation of a German sound, the English sound closest to it is provided. An explanation of this is found in Chapter 1.

There are two appendices at the end of the book: a German/English dictionary and an English/German dictionary. These will come in handy when you need the translation of a specific word.

The Everything® German Phrase Book is a handy vehicle for learning German. It not only provides you with the most important grammatical functions of the language and a simple guide to German pronunciation, it also offers practical phrases for travel, shopping, dining, and business. With that said, it's time to begin.

Good luck! *Viel Glück!*

Acknowledgments

With much gratitude to Stefan Feyen for all his help and suggestions.

Chapter 1
Introduction to German

German is one of the Germanic languages of Europe and a close relative to English. German and English are brother and sister languages that were separated by time and geography during the migrations of the Anglo-Saxons. This means you can find many similarities of vocabulary and structure in the two languages. That's important: It makes learning German just a little bit easier. Some important facts about German will be introduced here, which will give you a basis for understanding the nature of the German language and what it will entail to learn to use it effectively.

...g German

...e English, German uses the twenty-six-letter alpha-...esigned by the Romans. Although most of the letters ...e the same visually, some have a distinctly unique pronunciation in German. Learning the German sounds of the alphabet is not a difficult task and will allow you to read words with ease.

Fact

In addition to the letters that are identical in both German and English, there are four letters that occur in German that do not in English. Three require the addition of an umlaut over a vowel: *ä*, *ö*, and *ü*. The fourth letter is a special compound of *s* and *z* and looks like this in the modern language: *ß*.

Once you are familiar with the characteristics of German pronunciation, you will find that you can pronounce nearly all words upon seeing them for the first time, because German is, for the most part, a phonetic language. Any variances from standard pronunciation will be pointed out and explained. In the Pronunciation Key you will find examples of how to pronounce individual letters, letter combinations, and special letters. The comparable English pronunciation of the letters and letter combinations is only a guide. To be absolutely precise about pronunciation, ask a German-speaking friend to say the sounds for you. However, the key will provide you with a close facsimile of German that will be understood by any German speaker.

PRONOUNCIATION KEY

German	English Representation Letter(s)	Comparable English Pronunciation
A	a	"a" in father
Ä	ay	"ai" in pain
AA	a	"a" in father
AI	i	"i" in like
AH	a	"a" in father
AU	ow	"ow" in how
ÄU	oy	"oy" in boy
B	b	"b" in baby
C	ts	"ts" in its
CH	h	"ch" in Scottish loch
CK	k	"ck" in sick
D	d	"d" in dad
DT	t	"t" in tot
E	ay	"ai" in pain
EH	ay	"ai" in pain
EI	i	"i" in like
EU	oy	"oy" in boy
F	f	"f" in fife
G	g	"g" in go
H	h	"h" in how
I	ee	"ee" in sleep
IE	ee	"ee" in sleep
J	y	"y" in yolk
K	k	"k" in kick
L	l	"l" in lull

..........m.....................	"m" in mom
............n.....................	"n" in nun
ᵕ ....o...................	"o" in open
OH ....o...................	"o" in open
OO ....o...................	"o" in open
Ö ....er..................	"e" in her
P...............p..................	"p" in pup
PF ....pf..................	"pf" in carp food
PH...........f....................	"ph" in photo
QU............kv..................	"kv" in sick vet
R...............r...................	"r" in red (guttural)
ER ....er..................	"er" in father (British)
S...............z..................	"z" in zoo
S...............s	(final) "s" in kiss
SS..............s	"ss" in kiss
ß...............s	"ss" in kiss
SCH ....sh..................	"sh" in shush
T...............t.....................	"t" in tot
TSCH..........ch	"ch" in church
TZ ....ts	"ts" in its
U...............oo	"oo" in moon
UH.............oo	"oo" in moon
Ü...............(ue).................	("oo" while saying "ee")
V...............f....................	"f" in fife
...............v	"v" in very
W..............v	"v" in very
X...............x...................	"x" six
Y...............(ue).................	("oo" while saying "ee")
Z...............ts	"ts" in its

ⓔ *Essential*

> Certain consonants that end a word and sometimes a syllable become voiceless. When a consonant is voiced there is resonation in the throat (b, g, z, and so on). When it is voiceless, there is no resonation in the throat. The German voiced consonants are d, g, w, and z. Their voiceless counterparts are p, t, k, f, and s.

Vowels

Pronouncing German vowels typically does not come easy to people who are used to speaking English. A few simple rules and some practice will make it easier.

Umlaut Vowels

Only three vowels can add an umlaut: *a, o,* and *u.* The umlaut is a signal that the sound of the vowel has been altered. In the case of *a* ("a" in father), the vowel *ä* is pronounced similar to the German letter *e* ("ai" in pain). When *o* adds an umlaut, it signals a new sound that does not exist entirely in English. The vowel *ö* is much like the *e* in the English word *her.* In making this sound, omit the *h* and the *r* and retain the sound of the vowel *e.* When you add an umlaut to *u,* you have a sound that does not occur in English. The vowel sound *ü* can be produced by pursing the lips to say the English sound *oo* (as in moon) but simultaneously pronouncing the English sound *ee* (as in seen).

Practice saying the following pairs of words.

Bar	*Bär*
schon	*schön*
fuhr	*für*

Note: Because there is no English equivalent of the sounds *ö* and *ü*, they will be represented in the chapters that follow by "er" and "ue" when the phonetic pronunciation is shown. In addition, the stressed syllable in a word will appear in capital letters: *Vater* (FAH tuh).

Short and Long Vowels

The vowels can be pronounced as either "short" vowels or "long" vowels. Short vowels tend to precede a double consonant, and long vowels tend to precede a single consonant. Look at the following examples and their pronunciation.

Short Vowels

Gasse ("a" in what)
fällen ("e" in get)
Kette ("e" in get)
Ross ("o" in toss)
können ("er" short e in her)
Butter ("oo" in look)
müssen ("eu" short oo
    with e-sound)

Long Vowels

Gas ("a" in father)
Käse ("ai" in pain)
geben ("ai" in pain)
los ("o" in open)
schön ("er" long e in her)
tun ("oo" in moon)
spülen ("eu" long oo with
    e-sound)

Consonants

German uses pronunciations and consonant combinations that are unfamiliar to native English speakers.

The Consonant Combination Ch

This consonant combination is often imitated by English speakers by the sounds *k* or *sh*. But it is really neither of those. To form the German *ch*, pronounce the sound *k* but open the throat slightly to permit a raspy rush of air to be exhaled. This requires considerable practice for English speakers—except for the Scottish, who have a similar sound in Scottish words such as *loch*, which means lake.

Practice saying the following words.

ich
ach
hoch
such

The Letter R

The German letter *r* is pronounced in two different ways, depending upon the geographical region. The German language is used not only in Germany, but also in Austria, Switzerland, and Liechtenstein. In some areas, particularly in the south, the sound *r* is a rolled *r* as heard in Italian or Russian. This sound is made by "flapping" a *d* on the palate of the mouth with the tongue.

The second *r* is often more difficult for English speakers. This sound is made at the back of the throat where the

German *ch* sound is made. Pronounce the *ch* sound and hold the final aspiration (a raspy rush of exhaled air). The point where that sound is made is where the German *r* is made. Without moving the jaw, change the sound *ch* to *r* by saying "ra." This can be done by slowly saying "ach ra." To become proficient using this sound will require regular practice, but in time you will find that you are using both the *ch* and the German *r* comfortably.

Many German words end in *er*. This combination of letters is similar to the final *er* in an English word as it is pronounced in Britain, for example, "father" is pronounced more like *fath-uh*. This British *er* is similar to the German final *er*.

Practice saying the following words.

rot	*Ring*
dort	*Karl*
Mutter	*Bruder*

The Letter Z

English has the sound of the German *z* at the end of words or syllables, but in English it is most often written as *ts* or *tz*. In German the final *z* is pronounced in the same way. The German word for "felt" is *Filz* and is pronounced "filts." This sound can also occur in the middle of a word, for example: *heizen*, pronounced "hytsen," which means "to heat." Unlike English, German also uses this sound to begin words. For example, *Zelt* is pronounced "tselt" and means "tent." The combination *tz* also exists in German, but it is found only at the end of words or between syllables, for example: *Fritz*, a name, and *blitzen*, "to flash lightning."

Practice saying the following words.

Zeit	*Zoo*
Harz	*Hitze*

The Letters Sp and St

The letter combinations *sp* and *st* have a unique pronunciation, especially when they begin a word or syllable. They are pronounced as if they begin with *sh*. Therefore, *Sport* is pronounced as "shport." *Stein* is pronounced as "shtine."

Practice saying the following words.

Spende	*sprich*
Stil	*Stadt*

German Dialects

Just like English, German has regional differences not only of pronunciation but also of vocabulary. In English, for example, whether you will say "corn on the cob" or "roasting ears" depends upon where you live. The same occurs in German vocabulary as well as in pronunciation. In the north of Germany near Hamburg, for example, it is common to hear the letter combinations *sp* and *st* pronounced differently from the rest of Germany: The *sh* sound is not used, therefore, *Sport* is pronounced "sport" and *Stein* is pronounced "stine."

Contractions

German contractions occur when combining a preposition and a definite article. However, an apostrophe is not used in contractions, for example, *in das* (in the) becomes *ins*, *zu der* (to the) becomes *zur*, and *von dem* (from the) becomes *vom*.

COMMON CONTRACTIONS

an das................ *ans*........................ at the, or to the
an dem .... *am* .... at the
auf das.............. *aufs*...................... on the
in dem................ *im* .... in the
zu dem................ *zum* .... to the
bei dem.............. *beim* .... by the
für das................ *fürs* .... for the
um das................ *ums* .... around the

Apostrophes are used in German to show that a letter has been left out of a word. A common expression that illustrates this is *wie geht's*, which asks "how are you?" In this expression the letter *e* has been dropped from the word *es* and replaced by an apostrophe.

Capitalization

German and English differ somewhat in how they capitalize nouns and adjectives. In German, all nouns are capitalized whether they are proper or common. The adjectives of proper nouns are not capitalized unless they are in an official name or title. Let's look at some examples:

Common Noun	English
Land	country
Schwester	sister
Haus	house

Proper Noun	Adjective	English
Amerika	*amerikanisch*	America/American
Deutschland	*deutsch*	Germany/German
England	*englisch*	England/English

Cognates

Cognates are words that are identical in both German and English (and often in other languages). Sometimes they are identical except for a letter change that is characteristic of the language. For example, *korrekt* is the German version of correct and uses the letter *k* where in English a *c* is used. If the German used *c*, the word would be pronounced radically differently. Look at the following list of cognates and take note of the German words that have a change of a letter to conform to German pronunciation.

Noun	Adjective
Automobil	*abstrakt*
Akzent	*aktiv*
Artist	*blind*
Baby	*effektiv*
Chance	*fair*
Diplomat	*innovativ*
Elefant	*historisch*

Hardware	*kommunistisch*
Kapitalist	*kritisch*
Konferenz	*lyrisch*
Manager	*mechanisch*
Name	*national*
Optimist	*negativ*
Party	*offensiv*
Pessimist	*politisch*
Pilot	*positiv*
Präsident	*relativ*
Problem	*rhythmisch*
Professor	*romantisch*
Restaurant	*solid*
Service	*sozialistisch*
Statistik	*strikt*
System	*total*

Can you guess the English meaning of the following words?

Familie	*Gitarre*
Natur	*perfekt*
attraktiv	*nervös*
Kaffee	*populär*

Patterns of Cognates

Certain cognates occur in groups that conform to patterns. Two large groups of such English words are nouns that end in –*ion* and –*y*. Another large category is a group of English adjectives that end in –*ic* or –*ical*. In German, the endings for these cognates are –*ion*, –*ie*, and –*isch*.

Nouns Ending in –ion	Nouns Ending in –ie	Adjectives Ending in –isch
Position	Philosophie	philosophisch
Situation	Psychologie	psychologisch
Spekulation	Therapie	therapeutisch
Tradition	Melodie	melodisch
Aversion	Astronomie	astronomisch
Dekoration	Harmonie	harmonisch
Formation	Anatomie	anatomisch
Information	Psychiatrie	psychiatrisch
Inspektion	Kolonie	bibliographisch
Koalition	Fotografie	fotografisch
Konstitution	Epidemie	epidemisch
Reservation	Biologie	biologisch
Revolution	Geographie	geographisch
Ventilation	Geologie	geologisch
Vibration	Archäologie	archäologisch

 **Question?**

How do I know whether I'm pronouncing German words correctly?
By using this guide, you can pronounce German words in such a way that German speakers will understand you. To develop a good accent, you should take a class, purchase some audio tools, or work with a native speaker.

Words Common to German and English

Since German and English are languages in the same Germanic group, they have many words in common. Some are almost identical and have an identical meaning in both languages. Others have a slight spelling difference, and still others are used for completely different meanings in the two languages and often are similar only in the smallest of degrees. Let's look at some examples.

PEOPLE

German	Comparable English	Modern English
Bruder	brother	brother
Gärtner	gardener	gardener
Knabe	knave	boy, lad
Mann	man	man, husband
Mutter	mother	mother
Onkel	uncle	uncle
Schwester	sister	sister
Sohn	son	son
Tochter	daughter	daughter
Vater	father	father

ANIMALS

German	Comparable English	Modern English
Affe	ape	ape, monkey
Frosch	frog	frog
Kalb	calf	calf

Kuh	cow	cow
Lamm	lamb	lamb
Maus	mouse	mouse
Schaf	sheep	sheep
Schwein	swine	swine, pig
Spinne	spinner	spider
Ratte	rat	rat
Tier	deer	animal

COLORS

German	Modern English
blau	blue
braun	brown
grau	gray
grün	green
rot	red
weiß	white

MISCELLANEOUS

German	Modern English
alt	old
Arm	arm
beginn	begin
bei	by
Brot	bread
Feld	field
fett	fat
Finger	finger
frisch	fresh

	foot
ꞁb	grave
Ɡut	good
halt	hold
hart	hard
Haus	house
ist	is
jung	young
kalt	cold
komm	come
mach	make
Milch	milk
Mond	moon
sing	sing
Sonne	sun
wann	when
warm	warm
Wetter	weather
Wolle	wool

Chapter 2
German Grammar Basics

This book provides ready-to-use lists of vocabulary and phrases for every situation. But still it's important to know why you're saying something in a specific way, so you can reuse a phrase in a new form that conforms to a new situation. This chapter is an introduction to the basics of German grammar. Grammatical structures will be explained and examples provided to illustrate how those structures function. When you finish these mini-lessons, you will have the the basic skills for saying things in German with accuracy.

...nd Nouns

...nglish names, German names tend to refer to ...ales or females. As time goes by, some names are ... less and less frequently because they are considered ...d-fashioned. At other times, new names become popular because they are the latest fad. But all in all, there are certain German names that are traditional and retain their popularity for long periods of time. Let's look at some traditional male German names.

Friedrich	Helmut
Hermann	Johann
Karl	Reinhardt
Wolfgang	

Here are some traditional names for females.

Charlotte	Gretchen
Helga	Ingrid
Klara	Luise
Marianne	

Some names for men and women come from foreign sources and are often in fashion for just a short time. For example:

Boris	Jens
Sabine	Sonja

Surnames

When using a person's surname, you shoul[...]
it by the title *Herr* (Mr.) for a man and *Frau* (Mrs., [...]
a woman.

Herr Schneider	*Herr Braun*
Frau Benz	*Frau Keller*

 Fact

The title *Fräulein* (Miss) was used quite commonly in the past to refer to a single woman. But just as the women's movement created cultural changes in the English-speaking world, so too did those changes occur in Germany. It is now taboo to use *Fräulein*. All women are addressed by *Frau*.

Professional titles are used much the same in German as in English. They do not usually identify the gender of the person addressed.

Professor Schmidt	*Doktor Brenner*

When speaking to a professional, the titles *Herr* and *Frau* are used when the last name is omitted and the gender of the person is identified.

Herr Professor	*Frau Professor*
Frau Doktor	*Herr Lehrer* (teacher)

and Gender

> are words that represent a person, an object,
an idea or concept. Boy, pencil, and education
examples of nouns. In English, the gender of a noun
masculine if it refers to males, feminine if it refers to
females, and neuter if it refers to inanimate objects. German is somewhat different. Many nouns that refer to males and females are masculine and feminine respectively. But many other nouns that refer to inanimate objects are masculine or feminine, and still other nouns that refer to living people are neuter. For example, *Mann* (man) and *Stuhl* (chair) are masculine. *Frau* (woman) and *Lampe* (lamp) are feminine. *Kind* (child) and *Haus* (house) are neuter.

It is important to know the gender of nouns. Gender determines how articles and adjectives are used with those nouns. It is wise to try to memorize the gender of a noun as you learn it. However, if you make a mistake and use the wrong gender, German speakers will still understand you and it won't be considered a major blunder.

It is often the form of a noun that determines its gender. Certain endings tend to signal a specific gender. For example, nouns that end in *–el, –en,* and *–er* tend to be masculine.

Onkel............	uncle
Mantel...........	overcoat
Wagen...........	car
Brunnen.........	well, fountain
Lehrer	teacher
Keller	basement, cellar

Nouns that end in *–ung, –heit, –keit, –in,* and *–ie* ar[
feminine.

Zeitung .... newspaper
Gesundheit ...... health
Einsamkeit ...... loneliness
Lehrerin .... (female) teacher
Industrie .... industry

Many that end in *–e* are also feminine.

Lampe .... *lamp*
Kreide .... chalk
Küche .... kitchen
Tante .... aunt

Nouns that end in *–chen* and *–lein* are diminutives
and are neuter.

Mädchen .... girl
Vöglein .... little bird

Sometimes a noun can have two genders. In such
cases, the noun usually has two different meanings. For
example, the masculine form of *See* means "lake." When
it's feminine it means "sea."

The Art of Articles

There are two kinds of articles in German: definite articles
and indefinite articles. Definite articles identify a specific

ɔun or group of nouns (the boy, the cars). Indefinite articles identify a noun or group of nouns in general (a boy, cars). German articles must agree with the noun in gender and number.

Definite Articles

The German definite article has three basic forms in the singular and one basic form in the plural, all having the meaning "the":

> *der*.... masculine/singular .. *der Mann* (the man)
> *die* .... feminine/singular .... *die Frau* (the woman)
> *das*.... neuter/singular .... *das Kind* (the child)
> *die* .... plural.................. *die Kinder* (the children)

 Alert!

Don't confuse the singular feminine article *die* with the plural article *die*. When nouns become plural, their definite article is *die*, no matter what gender they were in the singular. The following singular nouns *der Mann*, *die Lampe* and *das Haus* become *die Männer, die Lampen,* and *die Häuser* in the plural.

Indefinite Articles

The German indefinite articles correspond to the English articles "a" and "an" and are also used for the number "one." There are two forms of the German indefinite

article, and, like English, the indefinite form of th.
is a plural noun standing alone without any article.

> *ein* .... masculine/singular .... *ein Mann* (a man)
> neuter/singular .... *ein Kind* (a child)
> *eine*... feminine/singular ...... *eine Frau* (a woman)
> plural .... *Kinder* (children)

The indefinite article is also used to enumerate one of something: *Ich habe ein Buch und zwei Hefte.* (I have one book and two notebooks.) When referring to someone's profession with verbs like *sein* (to be) and *werden* (to become), unlike English, no article is required: *Ich bin Professor.* (I am a professor.)

Declensions

When nouns are used as the subject of a sentence, they are said to be in the nominative case. The nominative definite and indefinite articles are those illustrated in the previous section. However, the articles sometimes change depending upon how a noun is used in a sentence. For example, if a masculine noun is used as a direct object in a sentence, it is in the accusative case and requires a change of the article: *Ich kenne den Mann.* (I know the man.) As direct objects, feminine, neuter, and plural articles require no changes.

Certain prepositions and other functions cause other changes. These changes are described as the dative case and the genitive case. These changes of the articles are

eclensions. Let's look at the declension of the
e articles.

	Masculine	Feminine
nominative	*der Garten*	*die Lampe*
accusative	*den Garten*	*die Lampe*
dative	*dem Garten*	*der Lampe*
genitive	*des Gartens*	*der Lampe*

	Neuter	Plural
nominative	*das Haus*	*die Lampen*
accusative	*das Haus*	*die Lampen*
dative	*dem Haus*	*den Lampen*
genitive	*des Hauses*	*der Lampen*

The indefinite articles follow a similar pattern.

	Masculine	Feminine
nominative	*ein Garten*	*eine Lampe*
accusative	*einen Garten*	*eine Lampe*
dative	*einem Garten*	*einer Lampe*
genitive	*eines Gartens*	*einer Lampe*

	Neuter	Plural
nominative	*ein Haus*	*Lampen*
accusative	*ein Haus*	*Lampen*
dative	*einem Haus*	*Lampen*
genitive	*eines Hauses*	*Lampen*

Accusative Case

Articles change to their accusative case form when the noun is a direct object. Ask "whom" or "what" of the verb in a sentence to identify the direct object. For example: "They kiss the girl." Ask, "Whom do they kiss?" The answer is "the girl"—the direct object. In German, the noun that is the direct object must appear in the accusative case:

Masculine: *Sie küssen den Mann.* (They kiss the man.)
Feminine: *Sie küssen die Frau.* (They kiss the woman.)
Neuter: *Sie küssen das Mädchen.* (They kiss the girl.)
Plural: *Sie küssen die Frauen.* (They kiss the women.)

Some prepositions signal that the noun following them must be in the accusative case. These include *durch* (through) *für* (for), *gegen* (against), *ohne* (without), and *um* (around).

Masculine: *Er arbeitet für den Mann.* (He works for the man.)
Feminine: *Er arbeitet für die Lehrerin.* (He works for the teacher.)
Neuter: *Er arbeitet für das Mädchen.* (He works for the girl.)
Plural: *Er arbeitet für die Schwestern.* (He works for the sisters.)

Dative Case

The dative case is used to identify the indirect object in a sentence. The indirect object is identified by asking "to whom" or "for whom" of the verb in the sentence. For example: "I give the girl red roses." Ask, "To whom do I give red roses?" The answer is "the girl"—the indirect object. In German, the indirect object must be in the dative case:

Masculine: *Ich gebe dem Mann rote Rosen.* (I give the man red roses.)
Feminine: *Ich gebe der Lehrerin rote Rosen.* (I give the teacher red roses.)
Neuter: *Ich gebe dem Mädchen rote Rosen.* (I give the girl red roses.)
Plural: *Ich gebe den Mädchen rote Rosen.* (I give the girls red roses.)

Some prepositions are signals that the noun that follows them must be in the dative case. Some of these are *aus* (out [of]), *bei* (by, at), *mit* (with), *nach* (after), *seit* (since), *von* (from, of), and *zu* (to).

Masculine: *Ich spreche mit dem Lehrer.* (I speak with the teacher.)
Feminine: *Ich spreche mit der Mutter.* (I speak with the mother.)
Neuter: *Ich spreche mit dem Kind.* (I speak with the child.)
Plural: *Ich spreche mit den Lehrerinnen.* (I speak with the teachers.)

Genitive Case

The genitive case is used to show possession. In English, this is achieved by an apostrophe plus the letter "s" or with the preposition "of" (the man's book/the roar of the lion). In German, the genitive case replaces both forms of English possession.

Masculine: *Wo ist das Buch des Mannes?* (Where is the man's book?)

Feminine: *Wo ist das Buch der Lehrerin?* (Where is the teacher's book?)

Neuter: *Wo ist das Buch des Kindes?* (Where is the child's book?)

Plural: *Wo ist das Buch der Kinder?* (Where is the children's book?)

Some prepositions are signals that the nouns that follow them must be in the genitive case. Two of these are *während* (during) and *wegen* (because of). In a sentence, they are used like this:

Masculine: *Wo warst du während des Winters?* (Where were you during the winter?)

Feminine: *Wo warst du während der Woche?* (Where were you during the week?)

Neuter: *Wegen des Gewitters bleibe ich zu Hause.* (Because of the storm I stay home.)

Plural: *Wegen der Probleme bleibe ich zu Hause.* (Because of the problems I stay home.)

The indefinite articles function in the four cases in the same way as the definite articles. For example:

Sie küssen einen Mann. (They kiss a man.)
Wir arbeiten für eine Lehrerin. (We work for a teacher.)
Sie sprechen mit einem Kind. (They speak with a child.)
Das ist das Auto eines Lehrers. (That's a teacher's car.)

Although the use of German articles is quite different from English, you will discover with time and practice that these declensions will fall into place for you. Be patient. There is no need to absorb all these endings immediately, don't be afraid to experiment with them. And if you use the wrong case, German speakers will still understand you.

Verbs Perform the Action for You

A verb is the word that describes the action in a sentence. It can describe something that happens (I eat/we learn), movement to a place (he runs/she flies), or a state of being (they are sick/I become tired). German verbs have to be conjugated, meaning they require specific endings depending upon what subject is using them. This occurs in English, too, primarily in the present tense. For example, you say "I see" but "he sees." The third person singular in English requires an –s ending on most verbs. The verb "to be" has an even more complicated conjugation: I am, you are, he is, we are, they are. In the other tenses, English verbs tend not to have conjugational endings. In the past tense, all the persons have the same form: I had/he had, we spoke/he spoke. But the verb "to be" is an exception: I was, you were, he was, we were, they were.

German also has conjugational endings, but unlike English, these endings are required for all persons and in all tenses. The basic form of a verb is the infinitive. English infinitives begin with particle word "to," for example: to come, to sing, to have, to bring. In German, many infinitives end in *–en*, for example: *kommen, singen, haben, bringen*. Some infinitives end in *–n*: *sein* (to be), *tun* (to do).

In order to conjugate a German verb, you have to drop the infinitive ending (*-n* or *–en*) and add the appropriate endings. Those endings are determined by the number, person, voice, mood, and tense of the verb in a sentence. At first glance, you may feel that German conjugations are quite complicated, but you will discover that the conjugations follow very consistent patterns.

Number, Person, Subject Pronouns

In order to conjugate verbs, you need to be acquainted with the subject pronouns. Number refers to singular or plural. Person is defined as first person, second person, and third person. Therefore, subject pronouns are described as first person singular (I) and plural (we), second person singular and plural (you), and third person singular (he, she, it) and plural (they). The German subject pronouns are:

	Singular	**Plural**
1st person	*ich* (I)	*wir* (we)

2nd person	*du* (you)	*ihr* (you) / *Sie* (you)
3rd person	*er* (he, it)	*sie* (they)
	sie (she, it)	
	es (it)	

Essential

There are three words that mean "you" in German: *du*, *ihr*, and *Sie*. The pronoun *du* is singular and informal. Use it when speaking to children, family members, and friends. Its plural form is *ihr*. The pronoun *Sie* should be used when speaking on a formal basis to one person or to a group.

The verbs *duzen* and *siezen* are used when describing the kind of relationship you have with another person. *Wir duzen einander.* (Informal relationship: We say *du* to one another.) *Wir siezen einander.* (Formal relationship: We say *Sie* to one another.)

Replacing Nouns with Pronouns

When you replace a noun with a subject pronoun, the pronoun must be of the same gender and number as the noun it replaces. But remember that even inanimate nouns can be masculine or feminine, and some animates can be neuter, especially when they are diminutives (*das Mädchen, das Vöglein*). Choose the pronoun that replaces a noun carefully; inanimate nouns are replaced by "it" in English, but not necessarily in German.

Noun	Pronoun Replacement	English Translation
der Onkel (uncle)	*er*	he
das Land (country)	*es*	it
die Kinder (children)	*sie*	they
die Häuser (houses)	*sie*	they
der Stuhl (chair)	*er*	it
die Tante (aunt)	*sie*	she
die Kreide (chalk)	*sie*	it
das Kind (child)	*es*	he / she

All plural nouns, whether animate or inanimate, are replaced by *sie* (they).

> *Wo ist der Stuhl? Wo ist er?*
> (Where is the chair? Where is it?)
> *Wo ist Tante Luise? Wo ist sie?*
> (Where is Aunt Luise? Where is she?)
> *Wo ist das Buch? Wo ist es?*
> (Where is the book? Where is it?)

Many English sentences begin with the word "it" when "it" is not the replacement of a specific noun. In that kind of usage, "it" is called an impersonal pronoun. The German pronoun *es* functions in the same way.

> *Es ist kalt.* (It's cold.)
> *Es wird spät.* (It's getting late.)

:ndings Make the Difference

The conjugation of German verbs is a bit more complicated than the conjugation of English verbs. You'll notice that similar endings are used in all the conjugations. That's helpful; it means you can apply the same endings to new verbs as they come along. Let's look at the present tense of some frequently used verbs: *kommen, singen, sein,* and *haben.*

kommen (to come)

ich komme (I come)
du kommst (you come)
er kommt (he comes)
sie kommt (she comes)
es kommt (it comes)

wir kommen (we come)
ihr kommt (you come)
Sie kommen (you come)
sie kommen (they come)

singen (to sing)

ich singe (I sing)
du singst (you sing)
er singt (he sings)
sie singt (she sings)
es singt (it sings)

wir singen (we sing)
ihr singt (you sing)
Sie singen (you sing)
sie singen (they sing)

sein (to be)

ich bin (I am)
du bist (you are)
er ist (he is)
sie ist (she is)
es ist (it is)

wir sind (we are)
ihr seid (you are)
Sie sind (you are)
sie sind (they are)

haben (to have)

ich habe (I have)	*wir haben (we have)*
du hast (you have)	*ihr habt (you have)*
er hat (he has)	*Sie haben (you have)*
sie hat (she has)	*sie haben (they have)*
es hat (it has)	

There are three pronouns that are spelled alike. One is the third person singular pronoun *sie* that means "she" or "it." Since it is singular, the verb that accompanies it will have a third person singular ending: *Sie ist. Sie singt.* (She is. She sings.) Another *sie* is the third person plural pronoun that means "they." Since it is plural, the verb that accompanies it will have a third person plural ending: *Sie sind. Sie singen.* (They are. They sing.) The third *Sie* means formal "you" and is also used with a plural verb ending. It is distinguished from *sie* (they) by context. For example: *Herr Braun, sind Sie krank?* (Mr. Braun, are you sick?) *Wo sind die Mädchen? Sind sie krank?* (Where are the girls? Are they sick?) Another difference is that *Sie* (you) is always capitalized.

In Good Voice

Voice in German refers to the active voice and the passive voice. The active voice describes an action that is performed by the subject of the sentence, often on a direct object: John kisses Mary. The passive voice places the subject in a passive position in the sentence and makes the direct object the subject: Mary is kissed by John. Although some argue that using the passive voice in English is poor style, it is a high-frequency structure in German.

Getting in the Mood

Mood in German refers to the indicative mood, the imperative, and the subjunctive mood.

- The indicative mood is the most common way of making a statement. *Herr Braun ist krank.* (Mr. Braun is sick.)
- The imperative is a command. *Sprechen Sie Deutsch!* (Speak German.)
- The subjunctive mood describes a conditional idea or one that shows a cause and an effect. *Wenn er nur hier wäre.* (If only he were here.) *Wenn er hier wäre, würde ich mit ihm tanzen.* (If he were here, I'd dance with him.)

Tenses

The main tenses covered in this book are the present, past, and future tenses. They are formed much like English tenses. You have previously encountered some present tense examples with *kommen, singen, sein,* and *haben.*

The regular past tense in English ends in –ed. The German regular past tense ends in –*te.* For example: *Ich fragte ihn.* (I asked him.)

The German future tense is formed by the conju tion of *werden* plus an infinitive. For example: *Die Kinde werden ihn fragen.* (The children will ask him.)

Adjectives

An adjective is a word that modifies a noun or a pronoun. Just like English, German has two ways of using an adjective. Many adjectives follow a linking verb like "to be" or "to become" and are called predicate adjectives. *Frau Benz ist krank.* (Mrs. Benz is sick.) *Es wird kalt.* (It's getting cold.) Other adjectives can be placed before the noun. *Wo ist der kranke Mann?* (Where is the sick man?) Adjectives that are not predicate adjectives require endings. Adjectives of this type are:

- Possessive adjectives: *mein*, *meine* (my), *dein*, *deine* (singular informal your), *sein*, *seine* (his, its), *ihr*, *ihre* (her), *unser*, *unsere* (our), *euer*, *eure* (plural informal your), *Ihr*, *Ihre* (formal your), and *ihr*, *ihre* (their)
- Demonstrative adjectives: *dieser*, *diese* (this, these) and *jener*, *jene* (that, those)
- Interrogative adjectives: *welcher*, *welche* (which)

Der-words

This category of adjectives is named *der*-words because the adjective functions like the definite article, meaning that the gender of the noun is identified in the *der*-word. Some of the *der*-words are *dieser* (this), *jener* at), and *jeder* (each). Note that *jeder* is only used in the singular. When these adjectives modify a noun, they show the gender or plural number of the noun by their ending.

> **Masculine:** *der Mann, dieser Mann, jener Mann, jeder Mann* (the, this, that, each man)
> **Feminine:** *die Frau, diese Frau, jene Frau, jede Frau* (the, this, that, each woman)
> **Neuter:** *das Haus, dieses Haus, jenes Haus, jedes Haus* (the, this, that, each house)
> **Plural:** *die Kinder, diese Kinder, jene Kinder* (the, these, those children)

Ein-*words*

This category of adjectives is named *ein*-words because the adjective functions like the indefinite article, meaning that an ending is required only for the feminine and the plural. The *ein*-words are the possessive adjectives and *kein* (no, not any).

> **Masculine:** *ein Mann, dein Mann, ihr Mann, kein Mann* (a, your, her, no husband)
> **Feminine:** *eine Frau, seine Frau, Ihre Frau, keine Frau* (a, his, your, no wife)
> **Neuter:** *ein Kind, mein Kind, unser Kind, kein Kind* (a, my, our, no child)
> **Plural:** *deine Kinder, eure Kinder, ihre Kinder, keine Kinder* (your, your, her, no children)

Adverbs

Adverbs are used more simply than adjectives be
there are no endings to consider. An adverb that descr.
time precedes an adverb that describes manner (by car, b
bus, on foot). An adverb that describes manner precedes
an adverb that describes place. Adverbs modify verbs,
adjectives, and other adverbs.

> **Modified verb:** *Sie laufen <u>schnell</u>.* (They run fast.)
> **Modified adjective:** *Mein Vater ist <u>sehr</u> krank.* (My father is very sick.)
> **Modified adverb:** *Sie sprechen <u>zu</u> schnell.* (You speak too fast.)

Know Your Pronouns

You have encountered other pronouons besides subject
pronouns in the nominative case. There are also accusative pronouns, dative pronouns, reflexive pronouns, and
relative pronouns. The list may seem long, but all pronouns follow a simple and logical pattern.

Accusative Pronouns

The accusative case is required when a noun is a
direct object or when it follows an accusative preposition (*durch, für, gegen, ohne, um*). The same is true of
pronouns: They can be used as direct objects or can follow an accusative preposition. The German accusative
case pronouns are:

(me)

n (you [singular, informal])

nn (him, it)

sie (her, it)

es (it)

uns (us)

euch (you [plural, informal])

Sie (you [singular/plural, formal])

sie (them)

In a sentence, the direct object pronoun follows the verb.

Sie findet es. (She finds it.)
Er liebt uns. (He loves us.)
Ich kenne dich. (I know you.)

With prepositions, the pronouns appear like this:

Er arbeitet für euch. (He works for you.)
Sie kommt ohne ihn. (She comes without him.)

Dative Pronouns

The dative case is required for indirect objects and following a dative preposition (*aus, bei, mit, nach, seit, von, zu*). In a sentence, the indirect object pronoun follows the verb. The German dative case pronouns are:

mir (me)   *dir* (you [singular, informal])
ihm (him, it)   *ihr* (her, it)

ihm (it)   *uns* (us)
euch (you [plural, informal])
Ihnen (you [singular/plural, formal])   *ihnen* (them)

In a sentence, indirect object pronouns precede the direct object if it is a noun. Indirect object pronouns follow the direct object if it is a pronoun.

Ich gebe dir das Geld. (I give you the money.)
Ich gebe es dir. (I give it to you.)

With prepositions, the pronouns appear like this:

Helga spricht mit ihnen. (Helga speaks with them.)
Sie wohnen bei ihm. (They live with him [at his house].)

Reflexive Pronouns

German reflexive pronouns can be in either the accusative case or the dative case and resemble the accusative and dative pronouns closely. Only their function is different.

Accusative	Dative	English
mich	*mir*	myself
dich	*dir*	yourself (singular, informal)
sich	*sich*	himself, itself
sich	*sich*	herself, itself
sich	*sich*	itself
uns	*uns*	ourselves

	euch	yourselves (plural, informal)
ı	sich	yourself, yourselves (singular/plural, formal)
sich	sich	themselves

The reflexive pronouns are used when the subject and the object in a sentence are the same person or thing.

Sie kauft ihm eine Jacke. (She buys him a jacket.)
Sie kauft sich eine Jacke. (She buys herself a jacket.)

Verbs that usually require a reflexive pronoun are called reflexive verbs. Some of the most common ones are:

sich anziehen	to dress
sich ausziehen	to undress
sich duschen	to shower
sich freuen	to be glad
sich hinlegen	to lie down
sich rasieren	to shave oneself
sich setzen	to sit down
sich waschen	to wash oneself

When a reflexive verb is conjugated, the appropriate reflexive pronoun must be used.

ich setze mich	I sit down (I seat myself)
du setzt dich	you sit down (you seat yourself)
er setzt sich	he sits down (he seats himself)

wir setzen uns	we sit down (we seat ourselves)
Sie setzen sich	you sit down (you seat yourself/ yourselves)
ihr setzt sich	you sit down (you seat yourselves)
sie setzen sich	they sit down(they seat themselves)

Relative Pronouns

The German relative pronouns are *der*-words—the definite articles or *welcher*. Just like English relative pronouns, German relative pronouns link a relative clause to a main clause. This occurs when the same noun is in both clauses. Two sentences such as "He knows the man. The man bought my car." become one sentence: "He knows the man who bought my car." The English relative pronouns (who, whom, whose, that, which) can be replaced by either a definite article or *welcher*, which closely follow the *der*-word declensional pattern.

	Masculine	**Feminine**
nominative	*der/welcher*	*die/welche*
accusative	*den/welchen*	*die/welche*
dative	*dem/welchem*	*der/welcher*
genitive	*dessen*	*deren*

	Neuter	**Plural**
nominative	*das/welches*	*die/welche*
accusative	*das/welches*	*die/welche*
dative	*dem/welchem*	*denen/welchen*
genitive	*dessen*	*deren*

The relative pronoun that replaces a noun must be the same number, gender, and case as the noun. For example:

Wo ist der Mann, der Deutsch spricht?
(Where is the man who speaks German?)
Wo ist die Frau, die Deutsch spricht?
(Where is the woman who speaks German?)
Wo ist das Mädchen, das Deutsch spricht?
(Where is the girl who speaks German?)
Wo sind die Kinder, die Deutsch sprechen?
(Where are the children who speak German?)

If the relative pronoun in the relative clause is used as the subject, it will be in the nominative case. As a direct object or after an accusative preposition, it will be in the accusative case. As an indirect object or after a dative preposition, it will be in the dative case. The genitive case is used to show possession, where in English the relative pronoun can be "whose" or "of which."

Being Negative

Negation in German is very much like English. It can be done in two ways: by inserting the negative adverb *nicht* (not) or by using the *ein*-word *kein* as a modifier. For example:

Sie wohnt nicht in Berlin. (She doesn't live in Berlin.)
Er kommt nicht heute. (He's not coming today.)
Es gibt keine Milch. (There is no milk.)
Ich habe kein Geld. (I don't have any money.)

Fact

> There are other negative adverbs like *nicht*. They, too, follow the verb in a sentence. Some examples are: *niemals* (never), *noch nicht* (not yet), and *nicht mehr* (no more). Two negatives are the pronouns *niemand* and *nichts*: *Niemand wohnt hier.* (No one lives here.) *Ich verstehe nichts.* (I don't understand anything.)

Asking Questions

Just like English, German has more than one way to ask a question. Sometimes just intoning your voice while you make a statement is a question. Other questions require a yes or no answer. Still others begin with an interrogative word.

Yes or No Questions

When asking a question that can be answered by either *ja* (yes) or *nein* (no), invert the subject and the verb to make a question.

> **Statement:** *Er kommt um acht Uhr.*
> (He's coming at 8 o'clock.)
> **Question:** *Kommt er um acht Uhr?*
> (Is he coming at 8 o'clock?)
> **Statement:** *Deine Schwester singt gut.*
> (Your sister sings well.)
> **Question:** *Singt deine Schwester gut?*
> (Does your sister sing well?)

Using Interrogative Words

Interrogative words ask questions about specific elements in a sentence: how, when, where, why, who, what.

COMMON INTERROGATIVE WORDS

wer	who
was	what
wann	when
wo	where
wie	how
warum	why

A question that begins with an interrogative word requires the inversion of the subject and verb, just like in a yes-no question.

Statement: *Du hast kein Geld.*
(You don't have any money.)
Question: *Warum hast du kein Geld?*
(Why don't you have any money?)
Statement: *Er findet eine Zeitung.*
(He finds a newspaper.)
Question: *Was findet er?*
(What does he find?)
Statement: *Sie kommen um acht Uhr.*
(They're coming at 8 o'clock.)
Question: *Wann kommen sie?*
(When are they coming?)

Chapter 3
Essential German

This chapter provides you with some of the most essential German vocabulary for travelers. It includes practical phrases like "Do you speak English?" and "I don't understand" as well as polite phrases, yes and no, numbers, calendar vocabulary, and instructions for telling time.

Survival German

The following German phrases just might come in handy as you make your way into the German-speaking world. Refer to Chapter 1 and the Pronunciation Key. In the phonetics, the capitalized syllable is the stressed syllable.

I speak a little German
Ich spreche ein bisschen Deutsch.
eech SHPRECH eh ine BISS chen doitch

Do you speak English?
Sprechen Sie Englisch?
SHPRECH en zee ENG lish

What does that mean?
Was bedeutet das?
vuss beh DOIT et duss

How do you say . . . in German?
Wie sagt man . . . auf Deutsch?
vee zahkt munn . . . owf doitch

Repeat, please.
Wiederholen Sie, bitte!
vee duh HOLE en zee BIT teh

More slowly. One more time.
Langsamer. Noch einmal.
LUNG zah muh noch ine MUHL

I don't understand.
Ich verstehe nicht.
eech fair SHTAY eh nicht

I don't know. What?
Ich weiß nicht. Wie bitte?
eech VICE nicht VEE bit teh

E Essential

Don't be afraid to use the German you know and to experiment. Germans understand that foreigners can make errors in their language, but appreciate the effort when someone uses German. Besides, it's good practice and will give you the confidence to speak and be heard.

Language Basics

The following vocabulary is quite basic but very useful.

LANGUAGE BASICS

yes	*ja*	yah
no	*nein*	nine
OK	*OK*	OK
and	*und*	oont
or	*oder*	OH duh
but	*aber*	AH buh
who	*wer*	vare
what	*was*	vuss

when	*wann*	vun
where	*wo*	voe
where (to)	*wohin*	voe HIN
why	*warum*	vah ROOM
how	*wie*	vee

> The interrogatives *wo* and *wohin* can be translated into English as "where." But *wo* is used to ask where something is located: *Wo ist das Theater*? (Where is the theater.) And *wohin* is used to ask where someone is going: *Wohin fahren Sie*? (Where are you driving?)

Being Polite

It's just common sense to be polite when you're a guest in a country. Saying "please" and "thank you" are the essentials for being a good guest.

POLITE VOCABULARY

please	*bitte*
	BIT teh
thanks	*danke*
	DUNN keh
thank you	*danke schön*
	DUNK eh shern
thank you so much	*vielen Dank*
	FEEL en dunk

thank you very much	*danke sehr*	DUNN keh zare
you're welcome	*bitte schön*	BIT teh shern
it was my pleasure	*gern geschehen*	gairn gheh SHAY en
don't mention it	*keine Ursache*	KINE eh OOR zuch eh
pardon me	*Verzeihen Sie*	fare TSY en zee
excuse me	*Entschuldigung*	ent SHOOL dee goong
I'm sorry	*es tut mir Leid*	ess TOOT meer LITE
bless you (after a sneeze)	*Gesundheit*	gheh ZOONT hite
cheers	*Prost*	prohst

 Alert!

Use *Verzeihen Sie* to mean "excuse me" or "pardon me" in the sense that you are looking to be forgiven for an action. *Entschuldigung* is more an apology and is used when asking for someone's attention.

TITLES

Mr.	*Herr*	hare
Mrs., Ms.	*Frau*	frow

Please don't let me disturb you.
Bitte lassen Sie sich nicht stören
BIT teh LUSS en zee zeech nicht SHTER en

Enjoy your meal!
Guten Appetit!
GOOT en ah peh TEET

It's Time to Count

Do you remember the line from a children's rhyme that says "four and twenty blackbirds baked in a pie?" That will come in handy as you learn to use the German numbers between twenty and a hundred.

NUMBERS

one	*eins*	ince
two	*zwei*	tsvy
three	*drei*	dry
four	*vier*	fear
five	*fünf*	fuenf
six	*sechs*	zex
seven	*sieben*	ZEE ben
eight	*acht*	ahcht
nine	*neun*	noin
ten	*zehn*	tsayn
eleven	*elf*	elf
twelve	*zwölf*	tsverlf
thirteen	*dreizehn*	DRY tsayn
ourteen	*vierzehn*	FEAR tsayn
een	*fünfzehn*	FUENF tsayn

sixteen	sechzehn	ZEX tsayn
seventeen	siebzehn	ZEEP tsayn
eighteen	achtzehn	AHCHT tsayn
nineteen	neunzehn	NOIN tsayn
twenty	zwanzig	TSVUNN tsik
twenty-one	einundzwanzig	ine oont TSVUNN tsik
twenty-two	zweiundzwanzig	tsvy oont TSVUNN tsik
twenty-three	dreiundzwanzig	dry oont TSVUNN tsik

From twenty to a hundred, the number in the second position is said before the number in the first position (24): "four and twenty blackbirds" *vierundzwanzig Amseln*. The first number to do this is twenty-one; the last is ninety-nine.

NUMBERS 30 AND UP

thirty	dreißig	DRY tsik
forty	vierzig	FEAR tsik
fifty	fünfzig	FUENF tsik
sixty	sechzig	ZEX tsik
seventy	siebzig	ZEEP tsik
eighty	achtzig	AHCHT tsik
ninety	neunzig	NOIN tsik
100	hundert	HOON dairt
200	zweihundert	TSVY hoon dairt
1,000	tausend	TOW zent
3,000	dreitausend	DRY tow zent
1,000,000	eine Million	ine eh MELL ee own

2,000,000 ..... *zwei Millionen* .... tsvy MEEL ee own en
a billion....... *eine Milliarde* ..... ine eh MEEL ee ahr deh
a trillion ...... *eine Billion* .... ine eh BEEL ee own

Take care not to confuse the German *Billion* (trillion) with the English billion.

What Time is It?

German does not use A.M. or P.M. to designate time between midnight and noon and between noon and midnight. Instead, the 24-hour or military clock is used. That means that 2 A.M. is said as zwei Uhr, but 2 P.M. is said as vierzehn Uhr.

> What time is it? It's . . .
> *Wie viel Uhr ist es? Es ist* . . .
> vee feel OOR ist ess; ess ist

one o'clock .... *ein Uhr*
          ine OOR
two o'clock.......... *zwei Uhr*
          tsvy OOR
3:30.................... *halb vier*
          hulp FEAR
4:15 .... *Viertel nach vier*
          vier Uhr fünfzehn
          FEAR tel nahch fear/
          fear OOR FUENF tsayn

4:45	*Viertel vor fünf/*
	vier Uhr fünfundvierzig
	FEAR tel for FUENF/
	fear OOR fuenf oont FEAR tsik
5:10	*zehn (Minuten) nach fünf*
	tsayn [mee NOO ten] nahch FUENF
6:50	*zehn (Minuten) vor sechs*
	tsayn [mee NOO ten] for ZEX
7 A.M.	*sieben Uhr........*
	zee ben OOR
3 P.M.	*fünfzehn Uhr.....*
	fuenf tsayn OOR
6 P.M.	*achtzehn Uhr*
	ahcht tsayn OOR
noon	*Mittag*
	MIT tahk
midnight	*Mitternacht*
	MIT air nahcht

Ⓔ *Fact*

When stating a time in the P.M. hours, the designations of *Viertel* (quarter) and *halb* (half) cannot be used, and the hour is stated followed by the number of minutes. For example: *siebzehn Uhr zwanzig* (5:20 P.M.), *zwanzig Uhr dreißig* (8:30 P.M.), and *zweiundzwanzig Uhr fünfundvierzig* (10:45 P.M.).

The Calendar

The German calendar starts on Monday and is otherwise set up like the calendar that English speakers use.

Days of the week

Monday	*Montag*	MONE tahk
Tuesday	*Dienstag*	DEENS tahk
Wednesday	*Mittwoch*	MIT vawch
Thursday	*Donnerstag*	DAWN airs tahk
Friday	*Freitag*	FRY tahk
Saturday	*Samstag/*	ZAWN ah bent
	Sonnabend	ZAHMS tahk
Sunday	*Sonntag*	ZAWN tahk

Months of the Year

January	*Januar*	YAH noo ar
February	*Februar*	FAY broo ar
March	*März*	MAIRTS
April	*April*	ah PRILL
May	*Mai*	my
June	*Juni*	YOO nee
July	*Juli*	YOO lee
August	*August*	ow GOOST
September	*September*	zep TEM buh
October	*Oktober*	awk TOE buh
November	*November*	no VEM buh
December	*Dezember*	day TSEM buh

Chapter 4
Meeting People

As you travel through the German-speaking world, it will be important to know how to greet people and exchange pleasantries in the local language. Not only will this make your travels a lot easier, but it will also give you a greater insight into how people in other countries interact. The traveler who knows nothing about the local language misses out on so much. So, say hello and have a friendly chat with your hosts. It will make your journey that much more enjoyable.

.eetings

. is common courtesy in Germany to say hello to the clerk when you enter a shop or store. When you're finished browsing or shopping, it's customary to say goodbye.

Saying Hello

hello, hi.............................	*hallo*
	hAH low
good morning......................	*guten Morgen*
	gOO ten MORE gen
good day, hello....................	*guten Tag*
	gOO ten tahk
good evening......................	*guten Abend*
	gOO ten AH bent

Leave-takings

bye, so long........................	*tschüss*
	chuess
goodbye.............................	*auf Wiedersehen*
	owf VEE duh zane
good night	*gute Nacht*
	GOO teh nahcht
see you later	*bis später*
	biss SHPAY tuh
see you in a while.................	*bis gleich*
	biss glych
see you tomorrow	*bis morgen*
	biss MORE gen

goodbye (on the telephone)..... *auf Wiederhören*

owf VEE duh hern

When you ask "How are you?" you must take into consideration what kind of relationship you have with the person you are speaking to, formal or informal. In general, you can say:

Wie geht's?.................... vee gates

Another informal version that you would use with people to whom you say *du* is:

Wie geht es dir?.............. vee gate ess deer

The plural informal (*ihr*) question is:

Wie geht es euch? .... vee gate ess oich

And the formal singular or plural (*Sie*) is:

Wie geht es Ihnen? .... vee gate ess EE nen

Appropriate Responses

fine, well .... *gut*

goot

I'm doing well................... *Es geht mir gut.*

ess gate meer goot

not well........................... *nicht gut*
nihcht goot

not bad .... *nicht schlecht*
nihcht shlecht

rather well....................... *ziemlich gut*
TSEEM lich goot

very well......................... *sehr gut*
ZARE goot

I'm not doing well. .... *Es geht mir nicht gut.*
ess gate meer nihcht goot

Introductions

When meeting people for the first time, you must still be aware of the formal or informal relationship involved. This will determine the form of your questions and answers. When asking for or giving a name, there are two basic approaches for both the formal and informal.

What's your name? (formal)
Wie heißen Sie?
vee HY sen zee

What's your name? (informal)
Wie heißt du?
vee hysst doo

What is your last name? (formal)
Wie heißen Sie mit Nachnamen?
vee HY sen zee mit NAHCH nah men

What is your last name? (informal)
Wie heißt du mit Nachnamen?
vee hysst doo mit NAHCH nah men

Her name is . . .
Sie heißt . . .
zee hysst
Ihr Name ist . . .
ear NAH meh ist

His name is . . .
Er heißt . . .
air hysst
Sein Name ist . . .
zine NAH meh ist

My name is . . .
Ich heiße . . .
eech HY seh
Mein Name ist . . .
mine NAH meh ist

Pleased to meet you. (formal)
Es freut mich Sie kennen zu lernen.
ess froit meech zee KEN en tsoo LARE nen

I'd like to introduce . . .
Ich möchte . . . vorstellen.
eech MERCH teh FOR shtell len

Alert!

When asking for or giving a name, the verb *heißen* is commonly used. Its meaning is "to be called." Therefore, you are really asking, "How are you called?" *Wie heißen Sie? Ich heiße Thomas Keller.* "My name is (I am called) Thomas Keller."

The Verb *Haben*

Haben means "to have." It is a very useful, high-frequency verb. Besides being able to stand alone in a sentence, *haben* also acts as the auxiliary of other verbs. Let's look at some sentences with this important verb.

I have a problem.
Ich habe ein Problem.
eech HAH beh ine pro BLAME

He has three brothers.
Er hat drei Brüder.
air haht dry BRUE duh

Do you have a sister? (informal)
Hast du eine Schwester?
hahst doo ine eh SHVES tuh

Do you have your passport? (formal)
Haben Sie Ihren Pass?
HAH ben zee EAR en puss

The verb *haben* is often used in special expressions and idioms, in which the translation is not always "to have."

I'm hungry.
Ich habe Hunger.
eech HAH beh HOONG uh

I'm thirsty.
Ich habe Durst.
eech HAH beh doorst

She's homesick.
Sie hat Heimweh.
zee haht HIME vay

Is something the matter?
Hast du was?
hahst doo vuss

He's busy.
Er hat zu tun.
air haht tsoo toon

He's fed up with that.
Er hat das satt.
air haht duss sutt

Haben *in Other Tenses*

The verb *haben* is just as useful in the past and future tenses as in the present tense. Let's look at its conjugation.

Present/Past/Future

ich	*habe* [HAH be]
	hatte [HAH teh]
	werde haben [VARE deh HAH ben]
du..................	*hast* [hahst]
	hattest [HAH test]
	wirst haben [virst HAH ben]
er/sie/es..........	*hat* [haht]
	hatte [HAH teh]
	wird haben [virt HAH ben]
wir.................	*haben* [HAH ben]
	hatten [HAH ten]
	werden haben [VARE den HAH ben]
ihr.................	*habt* [hahbt]
	hattet [HAH tet]
	werdet haben [VARE det HAH ben]
Sie	*haben* [HAH ben]
	hatten [HAH ten]
	werden haben [VARE den HAH ben]
sie	*haben* [HAH ben]
	hatten [HAH ten]
	werden haben [VARE den HAH ben]

ⓔ *Question?*

In the future tense, do I have to place the verb that follows *werden* at the end of the sentence?
This is one of the areas where English and German are different. In the English future tense, the verb stands directly behind "will" or "shall." In the German future tense, the verb is the last element in the sentence. *Sie wird mit Frau Schneider sprechen.* (zee virt mit frow SHNY duh SHPRECH en) "She will speak with Ms. Schneider."

Nationalities and Languages

As you travel, you encounter many people from many different lands. It is only natural that you talk about where you come from or that you ask about someone else's country. The following list contains the nouns that describe nationality. The masculine form is given first and is followed by –in to indicate the feminine form (*der Amerikaner/die Amerikanerin*). Where the feminine is formed differently, the noun is written out completely.

	Masculine	**Feminine**
African	*Afrikaner*	-in
	ah free KAHN uh	in
American	*Amerikaner*	-in
	ah mare ee KAH nuh	in
Austrian	*Österreicher*	-in
	ER stuh ryech uh	in

Asian............	*Asiat*	*-in*
	AH zee aht	in
Belgian	*Belgier*	*-in*
	BELL ghee uh	in
Brazilian........	*Brasilianer*	*-in*
	brah zee lee AH nuh	in
Canadian.......	*Kanadier*	*-in*
	kah nah DEE uh	in
Chinese.........	*Chinese*	*Chinesin*
	chee NAY zeh	chee NAY zin
Dutchman......	*Niederländer*	*-in*
	NEE duh lend uh	in
Egyptian........	*Ägypter*	*-in*
	ay GUEP tuh	in
Englishman	*Engländer*	*-in*
	ENG lend uh	in
European.......	*Europäer*	*-in*
	oy roe PAY uh	in
Frenchman	*Franzose*	*Französin*
	frahn TSOE zeh	frahn TSER zin
German.........	*Deutsche*	*Deutsche*
	DOITCH eh	DOITCH eh
(East) Indian...	*Inder*	*-in*
	IN duh	in
Italian...........	*Italiener*	*-in*
	ee tah lee AY nuh	in
Japanese	*Japaner*	*-in*
	yah PAH nuh	in
Mexican........	*Mexikaner*	*-in*
	mex ee KAHN uh	in

Pole	*Pole*	*Polin*
	POE leh	POE lin
Russian	*Russe*	*Russin*
	ROOS eh	ROOS in
Spaniard	*Spanier*	*-in*
	SHPAH nee uh	in
Swede	*Schwede*	*Schwedin*
	SHVAY deh	SHVAY din
Swiss	*Schweizer*	*-in*
	SHVITSE uh	in

Ⓔ *Essential*

When using words of nationality in context, you do not have to use an indefinite article (a, an / *ein*, *eine*), as you do in English. "Are you an American?" *Sind Sie Amerikaner*? (zint zee ah mare ee KAH nuh) "No, I'm a Canadian." *Nein, ich bin Kanadier.* (nine eech bin kah NAH dee uh)

The Verb *Sein*

The verb *sein* (to be) is another important high-frequency verb that can stand alone in a sentence or be used as the auxiliary of other verbs. It is used with nouns, pronouns, adjectives, and a variety of adverbial expressions.

I am a German teacher.
Ich bin Lehrer für Deutsch.
eech bin LAY ruh fuer doitch

Are you sick?
Bist du krank?
bist doo krahnk

She is very pretty.
Sie ist sehr schön.
zee ist zare shern

Where are they?
Wo sind sie?
voe zint zee

They're at home.
Sie sind zu Hause.
zee zint tsoo HOW zeh

She's in Munich.
Sie ist in München.
zee ist in MUEN chen

He's over there.
Er ist dort drüben.
air ist dort DRUE ben

Sein *in Other Tenses*

The verb *sein* is just as useful in the past and future tenses as in the present tense. Let's look at its conjugation.

Present/Past/Future

ich	*bin* [bin]
	war [vahr]
	werde sein [VARE deh zine]
du	*bist* [bist]
	warst [wahrst]
	wirst sein [virst zine]
er/sie/es	*ist* [ist]
	war [vahr]
	wird sein [virt zine]
wir	*sind* [zint]
	waren [VAHR en]
	werden sein [VARE den zine]
ihr	*seid* [zite
	wart [vahrt]
	werdet sein [VARE det zine]
Sie	*sind* [zint]
	waren [VAHR en]
	werden sein [VARE den zine]
sie	*sind* [zint]
	waren [VAHR en]
	werden sein [VARE den zine]

The verb *sein* is used in many practical expressions.
For example:

What is your occupation?
Was sind Sie von Beruf?
vuss zint zee fone beh ROOF

How is the weather?
Wie ist das Wetter?
vee ist duss VETT uh

It's cold.
Es ist kalt.
ess ist kullt

She comes from Hamburg.
Sie ist aus Hamburg.
zee ist ows HAHM boork

Is that really necessary?
Muss das sein?
moos duss zine

What can I get you? (in a store)
Was darf es sein?
vuss darf ess zine

Family Members

Talking about family is another interesting way to share information about yourself while getting to know other people.

FAMILY VOCABULARY

aunt . . . . *eine Tante*
ine eh TAHN tuh
brother . . . . *ein Bruder*
ine BROO duh

cousin (male).........*ein Cousin*
        ine koo ZAN

cousin (female) ......*eine Cousine*
        ine eh koo ZEE neh

daughter...............*eine Tochter*
        ine eh TAWCH tuh

father ....*ein Vater*
        ine FAH tuh

granddaughter........*eine Enkelin*
        ine eh ENK ell in

grandfather ....*ein Großvater*
        ine GROSS fah tuh

grandmother..........*eine Großmutter*
        ine eh GROSS moo tuh

grandson..............*ein Enkel*
        ine ENK ell

husband...............*ein Mann*
        ine munn

mother.................*eine Mutter*
        ine eh MOO tuh

nephew...............*ein Neffe*
        ine NEFF eh

niece...................*eine Nichte*
        ine eh NICH teh

siblings ....*Geschwister*
        gheh SHVISS tuh

sister ....*eine Schwester*
        ine eh SHVES tuh

son ....*ein Sohn*
        ine zone

uncle	*ein Onkel*
	ine AWN kell
wife	*eine Frau*
	INE eh frow

Chapter 5
Airports and Hotels

Now that you know how to greet people and chat about the basics, it's time to board a plane and head for your destination. This chapter deals with the situations you might encounter at an airport or when checking into a hotel. The vocabulary will guide you in making reservations, buying tickets, boarding the plane, going through customs, and getting to your hotel.

Using *Ich Möchte*

Germans prefer to use a special verb form in place of "want." *Ich möchte* means "I would like" and is considered the polite way of requesting something.

What would you like?
Was möchten Sie?
vuss MERCH ten zee

I would like to buy an airline ticket.
Ich möchte ein Flugticket kaufen.
eech MERCH teh ine FLOOK ticket KOW fen

Many useful phrases can follow *Ich möchte* . . .

. . . to cash these travelers' checks.
. . . *diese Reiseschecks einlösen.*
DEE zeh RYE zeh shecks INE ler zen

. . . to change this into euros.
. . . *dies in Euro wechseln.*
Dees in OY roe VEX eln

. . . a train schedule.
. . . *einen Zugfahrplan.*
INE en TSOOK far plahn

. . . a room.
. . . *ein Zimmer.*
ine TSIMM uh

The conjugation of this verb in the present tense, all persons is:

ich möchte [MERCH teh]
du möchtest [MERCH test]
er, sie, es möchte [MERCH teh]
wir möchten [MERCH ten]
ihr möchtet [MERCH tet]
Sie möchten [MERCH ten]
sie möchten [MERCH ten]

The verb *wollen* (to want) is an acceptable alternative but is not as polite. In the present and past tenses, it is conjugated like this:

Present/Past

ich	*will* [vill]
	wollte [VAWL teh]
du	*willst* [villst]
	wolltest [VAWL test]
er, sie, es	*will* [vill]
	wollte [VAWL teh]
wir	*wollen* [VAW len]
	wollten [VAWL ten]
ihr	*wollt* [vawlt]
	wolltet [VAWL tet]
Sie	*wollen* [VAW len]
	wollten [VAWL ten]
sie	*wollen* [VAW len]
	wollten [VAWL ten]

Verbs That Move You

Some verbs are called "verbs of motion" because they are used to describe getting from one place to another.

The Verb Gehen

The verb *gehen* means "to go" especially on foot. It is used when you are going short distances that can be reached by walking. Its present and past conjugations are:

Present/Past

ich	*gehe* [GAY eh]
	ging [ging]
du	*gehst* [gayst]
	gingst [gingst]
er, sie, es	*geht* [gayt]
	ging [ging]
wir	*gehen* [GAY en]
	gingen [GING en]
ihr	*geht* [gayt]
	gingt [gingt]
Sie	*gehen* [GAY en]
	gingen [GING en]
sie	*gehen* [GAY en]
	gingen [GING en]

Where are you going?
Wohin gehen Sie?
voe HIN GAY en zee

I'm going home.
Ich gehe nach Hause.
eech GAH eh nahch HOW zeh

We're going to the hotel.
Wir gehen zum Hotel.
veer GAH en tsoom HOE tel

The Verb Fahren

The verb *fahren* means "to go" or "to drive" and is used to describe getting someplace by vehicle. Its present and past conjugations are:

Present/Past

ich	*fahre* [FAHR eh]
	fuhr [foor]
du........................	*fährst* [fairst]
	fuhrst [foorst]
er, sie, es	*fährt* [fairt]
	fuhr [foor]
wir........................	*fahren* [FAHR en]
	fuhren [FOOR en]
ihr........................	*fahrt* [fahrt]
	fuhrt [foort]
Sie	*fahren* [FAHR en]
	fuhren [FOOR en]
sie	*fahren* [FAHR en]
	fuhren [FOOR en]

Where are they going?
Wohin fahren sie?
voe HIN FAHR en zee

They're going to the city.
Sie fahren in die Stadt.
zee FAHR en in dee SHTUTT

Are you going by bus or by train?
Fahren Sie mit dem Bus oder mit dem Zug?
FAHR en zee mitt dame boos OH duh mitt dame tsook

My husband drives very well.
Mein Mann fährt sehr gut.
mine munn fairt zare goot

Ⓔ *Fact*

Use the verb *fahren* to say that you are riding on or operating a vehicle: *Ich fahre ein Moped.* (I'm riding a moped.) *Er fährt ein Motorboot.* (He's driving a motorboot.)

The Verb Fliegen

The verb *fliegen* means "to fly." Its present and past tense conjugations are:

Present/Past

ich	*fliege* [FLEEG eh]
	flog [flohk]
du	*fliegst* [fleegst]
	flogst [flohkst]
er, sie, es	*fliegt* [fleekt]
	flog [flohk]
wir	*fliegen* [FLEEG en]
	flogen [FLOHG en]
ihr	*fliegt* [fleekt]
	flogt [flohkt]
Sie	*fliegen* [FLEEG en]
	flogen [FLOHG en]
sie	*fliegen* [FLEEG en]
	flogen [FLOHG en]

Are you flying to Rome?
Fliegt ihr nach Rom?
fleekt eer nahch rome

No, we're flying to Munich.
Nein, wir fliegen nach München.
nine veer FLEEG en nahch MUEN chen

A lot of birds are flying over the lake.
Viele Vögel fliegen über dem See.
FEE leh FER ghell FLEEG en UE buh dame zay

🄴 Essential

Unlike English, German is specific about how you get to a place: on foot, in a vehicle, or in a plane. So use *gehen*, *fahren*, and *fliegen* to give the appropriate meaning you want. If you asked someone in German whether he's going to Japan, you wouldn't use the verb *gehen*—"going on foot." You'd use *fliegen*—"to fly."

Airport and Flight Vocabulary

Now that you're equipped with some essential verbs, you're ready to take a trip to Germany. You can make reservations, buy your ticket, and get on a plane. Here are some German phrases that will come in handy.

PEOPLE, PLACES, AND THINGS

arrivals .... *Ankünfte*
　　　　　　　　　　AHN kuenf teh
airplane .... *das Flugzeug*
　　　　　　　　　　duss FLOOK tsoik
airport .... *der Flughafen*
　　　　　　　　　　dair FLOOK hah fen
baggage .... *das Gepäck*
　　　　　　　　　　duss gheh PECK
boarding pass .... *die Bortkarte, Einsteigekarte*
　　　　　　　　　　dee BOHRT kahr teh,
　　　　　　　　　　die AYN schteeg kahr teh

carry-on luggage...... *das Handgepäck*
duss HAHNT
gheh peck

checked luggage...... *das abgefertigte Gepäck*
duss AHP gheh fair tick teh
gheh PECK

check-in desk.......... *der Abfertigungsschalter*
dair AHP fair tee goongs shull tuh

departures .... *Abflüge*
AHP flue gheh

duty-free shop .... *der Duty-free-Shop*
dair doo tee FREE shawp

early .... *früh*
frueh

identification .... *der Ausweis*
dair OWS vice

late .... *spät*
shpate

passenger .... *der Fluggast, Passagier*
dair FLOOK gust, pah sah ZHEER

passport................ *der Pass*
dair puss

pilot..................... *der Pilot*
dair pee LOTE

security check......... *die Sicherheitskontrolle*
dee ZICH uh hites kawn traw leh

shuttle .... *der Pendelbus*
dair PENN dell boos

steward(ess) .... *der Steward, die Stewardess*
dair STOO art, dee STOO ahr dess

visa...................... *das Visum*
duss VEE zoom

TICKET INFORMATION

airline................... *die Fluggesellschaft*
dee FLOOK gheh zell shuft

economy (coach)
class .... *die zweite Klasse*
dee TSVY teh KLUSS eh

first class .... *die erste Klasse*
dee AIR steh KLUSS eh

flight .... *der Flug*
dair flook

gate .... *der Flugsteig*
dair FLOOK shtike

one-way ticket......... *das einfache Flugticket*
duss INE fahch eh
FLOOK ticket

plane ticket .... *das Flugticket*
duss FLOOK ticket

round-trip ticket....... *die Hin-und-Rückflugkarte*
die hin oont RUEK flook-
kahr teh

stopover .... *die Zwischenlandung*
dee TSVISH en lun doong

terminal .... *der Terminal*
dair tare mee NAHL

TRAVEL VERBS

to board	*an Bord des Flugzeugs gehen,*
	ins Flugzeug einsteigen
	ahn bohrt dess FLOOK tsoiks
	GAH en, ins FLOOK tsoyk
	INE shty ghen
to buy a ticket	*ein Flugticket kaufen*
	ine FLOOK ticket KOW fen
to check bags..........	*das Gepäck aufgeben*
	duss gheh PECK OWF gay ben
to make a	
reservation.............	*eine Reservierung machen*
	ine eh ray zare VEER oong
	MACH en
to sit down	*sich hinsetzen*
	zeech HIN zetz en
to take off	*starten*
	SHTAHR ten

🄴 Fact

These verbs and verb phrases are in the infinitive form and can be used with the conjugations of other verbs you have learned. For example, *Ich möchte ein Flugticket kaufen.* (I'd like to buy a plane ticket.) *Sie wird eine Reservierung machen.* (She will make a reservation.)

.gage Claim, Immigration,
.d Customs

When you arrive at your destination, you will need to get your luggage and go through immigration and customs. You'll find this vocabulary helpful.

ARRIVALS AND BAGGAGE

to land..............	*landen*
	LUN den
arrivals	*Ankünfte*
	AHN kuenf teh
baggage claim......	*die Gepäckausgabe*
	dee gheh PECK ows gah beh
My luggage is	
missing	*Mein Gepäck ist verloren gegangen.*
	mine gheh PECK ist fare LORE en
	gheh GAHNG en

IMMIGRATION AND CUSTOMS

immigration.........	*die Passkontrolle*
	dee PUSS kawn trawl eh
immigration form..	*das Passkontrollformular*
	duss PUSS kawn trawl fore moo LAHR
last name...........	*der Nachname, Familienname*
	dair NAHCH nah meh,
	fah MEE lee en nah meh
first name	*der Vorname*
	dair FORE nah meh
customs	*der Zoll, die Zollkontrolle*
	dair tsawl, dee tsawl kawn TRAWL eh

nothing to
declare .... *nichts zu erklären*
               nichts tsoo air KLARE en

customs
declaration form ... *die Zollerklärung*
               dee TSAWL air klare oong

Here's my
passport. .... *Hier ist mein Pass.*
               heer ist mine puss

I have a visa......... *Ich habe ein Visum.*
               eech HAH beh ine VEE zoom

I don't have
a visa................ *Ich habe kein Visum.*
               eech HAH beh kine VEE zoom

I would like
to declare .... *Ich möchte . . . verzollen.*
               eech MERCH teh fare TSAWL en

At the Hotel

You've arrived! Now you need a place to clean up, rest, and unpack your things. The following words and phrases will be helpful for getting the accommodations you want.

Ⓔ Essential

In some German hotels you have to specify what kind of room you want and with what kind of facilities. Rooms don't always come with a toilet, sink, and tub. In less expensive hotels you will share the bath down the hall with other guests.

Helpful Phrases and Vocabulary

I would like a room for . . .
Ich möchte ein Zimmer für . . .
eech MERCH teh ine TSIMM uh fuer

ICH MÖCHTE EIN ZIMMER FÜR . . .

one night	*eine Nacht*
	INE eh nahcht
two nights	*zwei Nächte*
	tsvy NEHCH teh
one person	*eine Person*
	INE eh pair ZONE
two people	*zwei Personen*
	tsvy pair ZONE en

I would like a room with . . .
Ich möchte ein Zimmer mit . . .
eech MERCH teh ine TSIMM uh mit

ICH MÖCHTE EIN ZIMMER MIT . . .

two beds	*zwei Betten*
	tsvy BET en
a double bed	*einem Doppelbett*
	INE em DAW pell bet
a shower	*einer Dusche*
	INE ehr DOO sheh
a bathtub	*einer Badewanne*
	INE ehr BAH deh vunn eh
a toilet	*einer Toilette*
	INE ehr toy LET eh

a television............*einem Fernsehen*
INE em fairn zay en
a telephone ....*einem Telefon*
INE em tale ay FONE
air conditioning ......*einer Klimaanlage*
INE ehr KLEE mah ahn lah gheh

Do you have . . . ? Is there . . . ?
Haben Sie . . . ? Gibt es . . . ?
HAH ben zee, geept ess

HABEN SIE . . ./GIBT ES . . .

an elevator............*einen Fahrstuhl*
INE en FAHR shtool
laundry service.......*einen Wäschedienst*
INE en VESH eh deenst
a hairdresser/
barber ....*einen Damenfriseur/Herrenfriseur*
INE en DAHM en free zeur,
HARE en free zeur
a parking lot/
garage ....*einen Parkplatz/eine Garage*
INE en PARK plutz
INE eh gah RAH zheh
a restaurant...........*ein Restaurant*
ine ress taw RAWNG
a pool.................*ein Schwimmbad*
ine SHVIMM baht

Naturally the word *Hotel* on a sign tells you where you are. But other words identify places for lodging as well:

motel ....das *Motel* (duss moe TELL)
hotel room with
breakfast.........*das Hotel garni* (duss hoe TELL
GAHR nee)
inn ....*der Gasthof* (dare GAHST hofe)
boarding
house.............*die Pension* (dee pahng zee OWN)
bed and
breakfast.........*Zimmer frei* (TSIMM uh fry)

About Your Stay

Now that you found lodging, you need some vocabulary for getting around the hotel, paying your bill, and requesting a wake-up call.

HOTEL VOCABULARY

hotel............................ *das Hotel*
                              duss HOE tell
accommodations...... *die Unterkunft*
                              dee OON tuh koonft
no vacancy .... *belegt*
                              bay LAYKT
first floor (US),
ground floor (UK)..... *das Erdgeschoss*
                              duss AIRT gheh shawss

second floor (US),
first floor (UK)............ *die erste Etage*

dee AIR steh eh TAH zheh

hallway .... *der Korridor, Flur*

dare koe ree DORE, floor

room .... *das Zimmer*

duss TSIMM uh

door .... *die Tür*

dee tuer

window .... *das Fenster*

duss FEN stuh

bed............................. *das Bett*

duss bett

pillow......................... *das Kissen*

duss KISS en

sofa .... *das Sofa*

duss ZOE fuh

wardrobe .... *der Kleiderschrank*

dare KLY duh shrunk

lamp........................... *die Lampe*

dee LUMP eh

bathroom .... *das Badezimmer*

duss BAH deh tsimm uh

lavatory...................... *die Toilette*

dee toy LET eh

towel .... *das Handtuch*

duss HAHNT tooch

Where is . . . ?
Wo ist . . . ?
voe ist

WO IST . . .

the elevator	*der Fahrstuhl*	
	dare FAHR shtool	
the laundry		
service.............	*der Wäschedienst*	
	dare VESH eh deenst	
the hairdresser/		
barber	*der Damenfriseur/Herrenfriseur*	
	dare DAHM en free zeur,	
	HARE en free zeur	
the parking lot/		
garage	*der Parkplatz/eine Garage*	
	dare PARK plutz, INE eh gah RAH zheh	
the restaurant.....	*das Restaurant*	
	duss ress taw RAWNG	
the pool	*das Schwimmbad*	
	duss SHVIMM baht	
the reception		
desk................	*die Rezeption*	
	dee ray TSEP tsee own	

I would like a wake-up call at 8 A.M.
Ich möchte um acht Uhr einen Weckanruf.
eech MERCH teh oom ahcht oor INE en
VECK ahn roof

What is checkout time?
Um wie viel Uhr muss man abreisen?
oom vee feel oor moos mahn AHP rize en

How much is it?
Wie viel kostet es?
vee feel KAWS tet ess

I would like to pay my bill.
Ich möchte gerne bezahlen.
eech MERCH teh GARE neh beh TSAH len

The bill is incorrect.
Die Rechnung stimmt nicht.
dee REHCH noong shtimmt nicht

I would like to pay . . .
Ich möchte . . . bezahlen.
eech MERCH teh bay TSAH len

ICH MÖCHTE . . . BEZAHLEN.

in cash..........................*bar*
                            bahr
with traveler's checks ....*mit Reiseschecks*
                            mit RYZE eh shecks
with a credit card.............*mit Kreditkarte*
                            mit kray DEET kahr teh

E Alert!

When checking into your hotel, ask whether they take credit cards and traveler's checks. Some small hotels, inns, and bed and breakfasts don't.

Chapter 6
Taking in the Town

Whether you plan to drive a rental car or use the local subway or streetcars, you need some vocabulary for transportation. In this chapter, you'll find the German terms for various types of transportation and useful phrases for getting that rental car and asking for directions.

Asking for Directions

Sometimes it's fun to wander the streets of a town or village and discover all kinds of interesting places. But if you're in a hurry, you probably ought to ask for directions.

> Where is . . . ? It's . . .
> *Wo ist . . . ? Es ist . . .*
> voe ist, ess ist

USEFUL VOCABULARY

left	*links*
	links
right	*rechts*
	rehchts
straight (ahead)	*geradeaus*
	gheh RAH deh ows
next to	*neben*
	NAY ben
in front of	*vor*
	fore
in back of	*hinter*
	HIN tuh
above	*oben*
	OH ben
below	*unten*
	OON ten
near	*nah*
	nah
far	*weit*
	vite

in the north	....	*im Norden*
		im NOHR den
in the south	....	*im Süden*
		im ZUE den
in the east	....	*im Osten*
		im AWS ten
in the west	....	*im Westen*
		im VESS ten

Alert!

When making requests, like asking for directions, remember to use the polite forms and survival German vocabulary in Chapter 3.

Places to Go

Here's some vocabulary that will help you ask for directions to some important places.

DESTINATIONS

bank	....	*die Bank*
		dee BUNK
church	....	*die Kirche*
		dee KIRCH eh
city hall	....	*das Rathaus*
		duss RAHT hows
currency exchange	....	*der Geldwechsel*
		dair GHELT veck sel

hospital..................	*das Krankenhaus*
	duss KRAHNK en hows
movie theater...........	*das Kino*
	duss KEE noe
museum.................	*das Museum*
	duss moo ZAY oom
park.....................	*der Park*
	dair park
pastry shop	*die Konditorei*
	dee kawn dee tore EYE
police station	*die Polizeistation*
	dee poh lee TSY shtah tsee OWN
post office...............	*das Postamt*
	duss PAWST uhmt
school	*die Schule*
	dee SHOO leh
theater..................	*das Theater*
	duss tay AH tuh

Other places you might like to go, including stores and businesses, are covered in Chapter 8.

Essential

Most cities have both a subway system (*die U-Bahn*) and a city and suburban train system (*die S-Bahn*). Look for the letter U on a sign to identify the entrance to the subway and the letter S that identifies the entrance to the city and suburban train.

Types of Transportation

Here are some useful words and phrases that deal with the various types of transportation.

TRANSPORTATION VOCABULARY

transportation .... *der Transport*
　　　　　　　　dare TRAHNS port

car...................... *der Wagen/das Auto*
　　　　　　　　dare VAH gen/duss OW toe

taxi..................... *das Taxi*
　　　　　　　　duss TAHK see

taxi stand.............. *der Taxistand*
　　　　　　　　dare TAHK see shtunt

train.................... *der Zug*
　　　　　　　　dare tsook

train platform......... *der Bahnsteig*
　　　　　　　　dare BAHN shtike

train station .... *der Bahnhof*
　　　　　　　　dare BAHN hofe

bus .... *der Bus*
　　　　　　　　dare boos

bus stop .... *die Bushaltestelle*
　　　　　　　　dee BOOS hult eh shtell eh

bus station .... *der Busbahnhof*
　　　　　　　　dare BOOS bahn hofe

subway .... *die U-Bahn*
　　　　　　　　dee OO bahn

subway station .... *die U-Bahn-Station*
　　　　　　　　dee OO bahn shtah tsee own

city and suburban
train . . . . *die S-Bahn*
                        dee ESS bahn

city and suburban
train station . . . . *die S-Bahn-Station*
                        dee ESS bahn shtah tsee own

bike . . . . *das Fahrrad*
                        duss FAHR raht

moped . . . . *das Moped*
                        duss MOE pet

boat . . . . *das Boot*
                        duss bote

Ⓔ *Alert!*

If you use the verb *fahren* with vehicles like those shown above, don't forget that there are two meanings for the verb. One says that you're traveling by some vehicle. The other says that you're driving that vehicle. *Ich fahre mit dem Bus.* (I'm traveling by bus.) *Ich fahre einen Bus.* (I'm driving a bus.)

Renting a Car

Public transportation is a convenient way to get around in a large city. But if you plan on traveling between cities or visiting sites out in the country, renting a car just might be the right thing for you.

I'd like to rent a car.
Ich möchte ein Auto mieten.
eech MERCH teh ine OW toe MEE ten

VEHICLE VOCABULARY

automatic
transmission .... *das Automatik-Getriebe*
                duss ow toe MAH teek
                geh TREE buh
economy car .... *der Economywagen*
                dare ay koe noe MEE vah gen
compact car .... *der Kompaktwagen*
                dare KOME pahkt vah gen
mid-size car........... *der Mittelgroßwagen*
                dare MIT ell grohs vah gen
luxury car............. *der Luxuswagen*
                dare LOOKS oos vah gen
convertible............ *das Kabrio*
                duss KAH bree oh
4x4 .... *mit Vierradantrieb*
                mitt feer raht AHN treep
truck .... *der Lastwagen*
                dare LAHST vah ghen

How much does it cost?
Wie viel kostet es?
vee feel KAWS tet ess

Do I have to pay by the kilometer?
Muss man pro Kilometer bezahlen?
moos mahn pro kee loe MAY tuh bay TSAH len

Is insurance included?
Ist die Versicherung eingeschlossen?
ist dee fare ZICH air oong INE gheh shlaw sen

I'd like to pay by credit card.
Ich möchte mit Kreditkarte bezahlen.
eech MERCH teh mit kray DEET kahr teh beh TSAH len

Where can I pick up the car?
Wo kann ich den Wagen abholen?
voe kahn eech dane VAH ghen AHP hoe len

When do I have to return it?
Wann muss ich ihn zurückbringen?
wunn moos eech een tsoo RUECK bring en

Can I return it to Berlin/Munich?
Kann ich ihn in Berlin/München abgeben?
kahn eech een in bare LEEN/MUENCH en AHP gay ben

Alert!

Cars in Europe usually have manual transmissions, so if you can't drive a stick shift, be sure to call around to rental companies to find out who offers cars with automatic transmissions.

Car and Driver

Here's some vocabulary that every driver needs when out on the road, filling up, and finding a parking spot.

DRIVING VOCABULARY

brake light.............	*das Bremslicht*
	duss BREMZ lihcht
brake...................	*die Bremse*
	dee BREMZ eh
driver	*der Fahrer*
	dare FAHR uh
flat tire/	
breakdown............	*die Panne*
	dee PUHN eh
gas, petrol.............	*das Benzin*
	duss ben TSEEN
gas pedal..............	*das Gaspedal*
	duss gahss pay DAHL
gas station.............	*die Tankstelle*
	dee TAHNK shtell eh
headlight	*der Scheinwerfer*
	dare SHINE vare fuh
high beam	*das Fernlicht*
	duss FAIRN lihcht
highway	*die öffentliche Straße*
	dee ER fent leech eh SHTRAH seh
super highway........	*die Autobahn, Landstraße*
	dee OW toe bahn, LUNT shtrah seh
hitchhiking............	*das Trampen*
	duss TRAHM pen

on the way .... *unterwegs*
OON tuh vakes

one-way street .... *die Einbahnstraße*
dee INE bahn shtrah seh

parking lot .... *der Parkplatz*
dare PARK plutz

regular gas .... *das Normalbenzin*
duss nore MAHL ben tseen

speed limit .... *die Geschwindigkeitsbeschränkung*
dee gheh SHVIN dih kites
beh SHRENK oong

steering wheel .... *das Lenkrad*
duss LENK raht

street .... *die Straße*
dee SHTRAH seh

toll .... *die Gebühr*
dee gheh BUER

traffic jam .... *der Verkehrsstau/der Stau*
dare fare KARES shtau/der shtau

traffic light .... *die Verkehrsampel*
dee fare KARES ahm pell

trip .... *die Fahrt*
dee fahrt

turn signal .... *der Blinker*
dare BLINK uh

windshield .... *die Windschutzscheibe*
dee VINT shoots shy beh

windshield wiper .... *der Scheibenwischer*
dare SHY ben vish uh

Ⓔ *Essential*

The German *Autobahn* is famous for its conve-
nience for getting across Germany quickly and eas-
ily. Although there are places on these roadways
that have no speed limit, newcomers should be
aware that there are also areas that have vigorously
enforced speed limits. Be sure to keep to the right
except when passing. That's a strict rule and the one
that permits the use of high speed.

Useful Driving Verbs

Here are some verbs essential for driving in Germany.

DRIVING VERBS

to accelerate..........	*beschleunigen*
	beh SHLOY nih ghen
to cross................	*überqueren*
	ue buh KVARE en
to drive	*fahren*
	FAHR en
to fill up (gas).........	*tanken*
	TAHNK en
to park.................	*parken*
	PAHR ken
to pass.................	*überholen*
	UEH buh hoe len

to slow down ....*verlangsamen, abbremsen*
fare LAHNG zah men, AHP brem zen
to turn ....*einbiegen*
INE bee ghen

Chapter 7
Time for Dinner

Going out for dinner can be a great experience and is an important part of enjoying a foreign culture. This chapter will present you with the most essential words and phrases for understanding a German menu and ordering correctly. *Guten Appetit!*

Eating Out

Here are some basic words and phrases that you'll find helpful when eating out.

AT THE RESTAURANT

restaurant ....*das Restaurant*
　　　　　　　　　　duss ress toh RAHNG

snackbar ....*der Schnellimbiss*
　　　　　　　　　　dare SHNELL im biss

kitchen ....*die Küche*
　　　　　　　　　　dee KUECH eh

dining room ....*das Esszimmer*
　　　　　　　　　　duss ESS tsimm uh

waiter..................*der Kellner*
　　　　　　　　　　dare KELL nuh

waitress................*die Kellnerin*
　　　　　　　　　　dee KELL nuh rin

cook ....*der Koch/die Köchin*
　　　　　　　　　　dare kawch/dee KERCH in

 *Question?*

How do I get my waiter's attention?
You can call to the waiter by saying "excuse me," *Entschuldigung* (ent SHOOL dee goong). Or you can ask for "service," *Bedienung* (beh DEEN oong).

MEALS AND COURSES

meal .... *die Mahlzeit*
dee MAHL tsite

breakfast .... *das Frühstück*
duss FRUE shtueck

lunch................... *das Mittagessen*
duss MIT tuck ess en

dinner.................. *das Abendessen/Abendbrot*
duss AH bent ess en/AH bent brote

snack .... *der Snack*
dare snack

appetizer, starter ..... *die Vorspeise*
dee FORE shpy zeh

soup.................... *die Suppe*
dee ZOO peh

main course .... *das Hauptgericht*
duss HOWPT gheh rihcht

salad .... *der Salat*
dare zah LAHT

dessert................. *der Nachtisch*
dare NAHCH tish

 Fact

In many parts of the German-speaking world, it is customary to have a late afternoon stop at a *Konditorei* (pastry shop) for some *Kaffee und Kuchen* (coffee and cake). Some people prefer a glass of wine over the coffee. You don't want to miss this experience.

What's on the Menu?

In order to choose correctly from a menu, you have to know what food items are available. Take a look at the following lists of different kinds of food.

FRUIT (*DAS OBST*)

apple	*der Apfel*
	dare AHP fell
apricot	*die Aprikose*
	dee ahp ree KOE zeh
banana	*die Banane*
	dee bah NAH neh
blackberry	*die Brombeere*
	dee BROME bare eh
blueberry	*die Heidelbeere/Blaubeere*
	dee HYE dell bare eh/BLOW bare eh
cherry	*die Kirsche*
	dee KEER sheh
grape	*die Weintraube*
	dee VINE trow beh
grapefruit	*die Pampelmuse*
	dee PAHM pell moo zeh
lemon	*die Zitrone*
	dee tsee TRONE eh
lime	*die Limone*
	dee lee MONE eh
orange	*die Apfelsine/Orange*
	dee ahp fell ZEE neh/oh RAHN zheh
peach	*der Pfirsich*
	dare PFEER zich

pear	*die Birne*
	dee BEER neh
plum	*die Pflaume*
	dee PFLOW meh
raspberry	*die Himbeere*
	dee HIM bare eh
strawberry	*die Erdbeere*
	dee AIRT bare eh

VEGETABLES (*DAS GEMÜSE*)

artichoke	*die Artischoke*
	dee are tee SHOKE eh
asparagus	*der Spargel*
	dare SHPAR ghel
bean	*die Bohne*
	dee BOE neh
carrot	*die Möhre/Karotte*
	dee MER reh/kah ROTE eh
cauliflower	*der Blumenkohl*
	dare BLOOM en kole
celery	*der Stangensellerie*
	dare SHTUNG en zell air ee
corn	*der Mais*
	dare mise
cucumber	*die Gurke*
	dee GOOR keh
lettuce	*der Kopfsalat*
	dare KAWPF zah laht
mushroom	*der Pilz*
	dare piltz

onion .... *die Zwiebel*
dee TSVEE bel

parsley................ *die Petersilie*
dee pay tare ZEE lee eh

peas................... *die Erbsen*
dee AIRP sen

potato................. *die Kartoffel*
dee kahr TAWF el

spinach .... *der Spinat*
dare shpee NAHT

tomato .... *die Tomate*
dee toe MAH teh

MEAT, FISH, POULTRY (*DAS FLEISCH, DER FISCH, DAS GEFLÜGEL*)

chicken............... *das Huhn/Hähnchen*
duss hoon/HANE chen

fish .... *der Fisch*
dare fish

ham .... *der Schinken*
dare SHINK en

herring................ *der Hering*
dare HARE ing

lamb .... *das Lamm*
duss lumm

lobster .... *der Hummer*
dare HOOM uh

mussels............... *die Muscheln*
dee MOO sheln

pork....................*das Schweinefleisch*
duss SHVINE eh flysh

roast beef ....*der Rinderbraten/das Roastbeef*
dare RIN duh brah ten/duss
roast beef

sausage................*die Wurst*
dee voorst

steak ....*das Steak*
duss steak

turkey..................*der Truthahn*
dare TRUEHT hahn

veal ....*das Kalbfleisch*
duss KULP flysh

venison ....*das Rehfleisch*
duss RAY flysh

MEAT PREPARATION

rare.....................*englisch gebraten*
ENG lish gheh BRAH ten

medium-rare/well....*halb durchgebraten*
hulp DOORCH gheh brah ten

well done..............*durchgebraten*
DOORCH gheh brah ten

DAIRY (*DIE MILCHPRODUKTE*)

buttermilk.............*die Buttermilch*
dee BOOT uh milch

butter ....*die Butter*
die BOOT uh

cream	*die Sahne*
	dee ZAH neh
sour cream	*der Sauerrahm*
	dare ZOW uh rahm
cheese	*der Käse*
	dare KAY zeh
cream cheese	*der Frischkäse*
	dare FRISH kay zeh
curd cheese	*der Quark*
	dare kvahrk
ice cream	*das Eis*
	duss ice
milk	*die Milch*
	dee milch
yogurt	*der Joghurt*
	dare YOGE hoort

DESSERT (*DER NACHTISCH*)

cake	*der Kuchen*
	dare KOOCH en
candy	*die Süßigkeiten*
	dee ZUESS ich kite en
chocolate	*die Schokolade*
	dee SHOE koe lah deh
cookie	*das Plätzchen*
	duss PLETZ chen
fruit	*das Obst*
	duss ohpst
ice cream	*das Eis*
	duss ice

pie	*der Obstkuchen*
	dare OHPST kooch en
pudding	*der Pudding*
	dare POO ding

AND SO ON (*UND SO WEITER*)

almond	*die Mandel*
	dee MUN dell
bread	*das Brot*
	duss brote
roll	*das Brötchen*
	duss BRERT chen
egg	*das Ei*
	duss eye
eggs	*die Eier*
	dee EYE uh
French fries	*die Pommes frites*
	dee pawm freet
jam	*die Marmelade*
	dee mahr meh LAH deh
ketchup	*der Ketschup*
	dare KETCH up
mayonnaise	*die Mayonnaise*
	dee mah yoe NAZE eh
mustard	*der Senf*
	dare zenf
pasta, noodles	*die Nudeln*
	dee NOO deln
peanut	*die Erdnuss*
	dee AIRT noos

pepper	*der Pfeffer*
	dare PFEFF uh
rice	*der Reis*
	dare rice
salt	*das Salz*
	duss zahltz
sugar	*der Zucker*
	dare TSOOK uh
toast	*der Toast*
	dare toste
vanilla	*die Vanille*
	dee vah NILL eh

Beverages

Pick out some drinks to go along with your food.

BEVERAGES (*DIE GETRÄNKE*)

beer	*das Bier*
	duss beer
cocktail	*der Cocktail*
	dare KAWK tail
coffee	*der Kaffee*
	dare kuh FAY
cocoa	*der Kakao*
	dare kah KAH oh
espresso	*der Espresso*
	dare ess PRESS oh
liqueur	*der Likör*
	dare lee KER

juice	*der Saft*
	dare zuft
lemonade	*die Limonade*
	dee lee moe NAH deh
milk	*die Milch*
	dee milch
mineral water	*das Mineralwasser*
	duss minn uh RAHL vuss uh
sparkling water	*das Selterswasser*
	duss ZELL tuss vuss uh
tea	*der Tee*
	dare tay
water	*das Wasser*
	duss VUSS uh
wine	*der Wein*
	dare vine
sparkling wine, German champagne	*der Sekt*
	dare zehkt

Fact

It is well known that Germans are fond of beer. That means that there are many local breweries and many kinds of beer to sample while you're enjoying a meal out. But don't be afraid to try the German wines as well. There are many fine Mosel and Rhine wines.

Dishes and Silverware

If you need to ask for another fork or a napkin, here's the vocabulary you'll need.

DISHES AND SILVERWARE

bowl	*die Schale*	
	dee SHAH leh	
cup	*die Tasse*	
	dee TUSS eh	
fork	*die Gabel*	
	dee GAH bell	
glass	*das Glas*	
	duss glahss	
highchair	*der Hochstuhl*	
	dare HOECH shtool	
knife	*das Messer*	
	duss MESS uh	
napkin	*die Serviette*	
	dee zare vee ETT eh	
plate	*der Teller*	
	dare TELL uh	
saucer	*die Untertasse*	
	dee OON tuh tuss eh	
spoon	*der Löffel*	
	dare LERF ell	
tray	*das Tablett*	
	duss tah BLETT	
wine glass	*das Weinglas*	
	duss VINE glahss	

bottle	*die Flasche*
	dee FLUSH eh
can, box	*die Dose*
	dee DOZE eh
jar	*der Topf/das Glas*
	dare tawpf/duss glahss

Ordering a Meal

With your new food and beverage vocabulary, you're
ready to talk with the waiter and order your meal.

USEFUL EXPRESSIONS

to be hungry	*Hunger haben*
	HOONG uh HAH ben
to be thirsty	*Durst haben*
	doorst HAH ben
to order	*bestellen*
	beh SHTELL en
to drink	*trinken*
	TRINK en
to eat	*essen*
	ESS en
check/bill	*die Rechnung*
	dee REHCH noong
menu	*die Speisekarte*
	dee SHPY zeh kahr teh
side order,	
a la carte	*a la carte*
	ah lah kart

fixed-price menu......*die Gedeck-Karte*
dee gheh DECK kahr teh

tip ....*das Trinkgeld*
duss TRINK ghehlt

tip is included ....*die Bedienung ist inbegriffen*
dee beh DEEN oong ist
in beh GRIFF en

tip is not
included...............*die Bedienung ist nicht inbegriffen*
dee beh DEEN oong ist nihcht
in beh GRIFF en

Ⓔ *Question?*

How do I know how much of a tip to leave my server?
Gratuity is usually taken care of for you in most restaurants. It is customary to include a service charge of 10 to 20 percent on your bill. But if you find that the service was especially good, it's proper to give your server a little extra.

What would you like? I would like . . .
Was möchten Sie? Ich möchte . . .
vuss MERCH ten zee, eech MERCH teh

What are you ordering?
Was bestellen Sie?
vuss beh SHTELL en zee

I'm ordering . . .
Ich bestelle . . .
eech beh SHTELL eh

How much does . . . cost?
Wie viel kostet . . . ?
vee feel KAW stet

Enjoy your meal!
Guten Appetit!
GOO ten AHP eh teet

No smoking!
Nicht rauchen! Rauchen verboten!
nihcht ROWCH en, ROWCH en fare BOE ten

No pets allowed.
Kein Zugang für Haustiere!
KINE TSOO gung fuer HOUSE teer eh

Dietary Restrictions

While you are traveling, you can still avoid the foods that
you normally would not eat at home. Use these German
phrases to explain your dietary restrictions.

I am . . .
Ich bin . . .
eech bin

USEFUL EXPRESSIONS

allergic to .... *allergisch gegen*
　　　　　　　　ah LARE gish GAY ghen
diabetic................*Diabetiker(in)*
　　　　　　　　dee ah BET ick uh (rin)
vegetarian............. *Vegetarier(in)*
　　　　　　　　veg eh TAHR ee uh (rin)

I'm on a diet.
Ich mache eine Diät.
eech MAHCH eh INE eh dee ATE

I can't eat . . .
Ich kann kein . . . essen.
eech kahn kine . . . ESS en

Chapter 8
Shopping and Services

Vacations are fun and keep you on the go. But certain things still have to be done: You have to keep your clothes clean and your hair trimmed. And you just might be getting tired of eating in a restaurant three times a day. So this chapter will introduce you to some phrases that are related to the stores and services you might need.

Stores and Businesses

Here's a list of stores and business that might come in handy.

DESTINATIONS (*ZIELE*)

bakery	*die Bäckerei*	
	dee beck eh RYE	
bank	*die Bank*	
	dee bahnk	
butcher shop	*die Fleischerei/Metzgerei*	
	dee flysh eh RYE/metz gheh RYE	
candy shop	*das Süßwarengeschäft*	
	duss ZUESS vahr en gheh sheft	
clothing store	*das Bekleidungsgeschäft*	
	duss beh KLY doongs gheh sheft	
dairy	*der Milchladen*	
	dare MILCH lah den	
department store	*das Kaufhaus*	
	duss KOWF house	
drugstore	*die Drogerie*	
	dee droe gare EE	
dry cleaner	*die chemische Reinigung*	
	dee KAME ish eh RINE ee goong	
fish market	*das Fischgeschäft*	
	duss FISH gheh sheft	
grocery store	*das Lebensmittelgeschäft*	
	duss LAY bens mit tell gheh sheft	
laundromat	*die Wäscherei*	
	dee vesh eh RYE	
shopping center	*das Einkaufszentrum*	
	duss INE kowfs tsen troom	

newsstand .... *der Zeitungskiosk*
dare TSY toongs kee awsk

outdoor market......... *der Markt*
dare mahrkt

pastry shop .... *die Konditorei*
dee kawn dee taw RYE

pharmacy/drugstore ... *die Apotheke*
dee ah poe TAY keh

shop..................... *der Laden*
dare LAH den

store..................... *das Geschäft*
duss gheh SHEFT

supermarket .... *der Supermarkt*
dare SOOP uh mahrkt

tobacconist .... *der Tabakwarenhändler*
dare tah BAHK vahr en hend luh

Fact

The *Apotheke* is one of the stores that is translated into English as "drugstore." But there is a difference between it and the *Drogerie*. In the *Drogerie*, you can obtain perfume, cosmetics, over-the-counter medicines, and various hygiene products. Some of the same products can be bought in the *Apotheke*. But the primary difference between the two is that the *Apotheke* has licensed pharmacists who can prepare prescription medicines and provide advice on their use.

Laundromat and Dry Cleaner

After traveling around for a few days, you're going to need to get your clothes cleaned. Here is some valuable vocabulary for solving this problem.

LAUNDRY VOCABULARY

to wash	*waschen*	VUSH en
to dry	*trocknen*	TRAWK nen
to dry clean	*chemisch reinigen*	KAME ish RINE ih ghen
bleach	*das Bleichmittel*	duss BLYCH mit tell
detergent	*das Waschmittel*	duss VUSH mit tell
dryer	*der Trockner*	dare TRAWK nuh
fabric softener	*das Weichspülmittel*	duss VYCH shpuel mit tell
rinse	*durchspülen*	DOORCH shpuel en
soap	*die Seife*	dee ZIFE eh
starch	*die Stärke*	dee SHTARE keh
washing machine	*die Waschmaschine*	dee VUSH mah shee neh

Hair Salon or Barbershop

You need to know how to tell the stylist or barber how you want your hair done. Familiarize yourself with the following vocabulary. It'll come in handy.

GROOMING VOCABULARY

to brush	....	*bürsten*
		BUER sten
to blow dry	....	*fönen*
		FER nen
to color	....	*färben*
		FARE ben
to curl	....	*locken*
		LAW ken
to cut	....	*schneiden*
		SHNY den
to perm	....	*eine Dauerwelle machen*
		INE eh DOW uh vell eh MAHCH en
to shave	....	*rasieren*
		RAH zee ren
to wash	....	*waschen*
		VUSH en
long	....	*lang*
		lung
short	....	*kurz*
		koortz
too cold	....	*zu kalt*
		tsoo kult
too hot	....	*zu heiß*
		tsoo hice

hair style .... *die Frisur*
                dee free ZOOR
hair stylist .... *der Friseur/die Friseuse*
                dare free ZER/dee free ZER zeh

(E) Fact

If you bring along your own electrical appliances, such as a hair dryer or shaver, on your trip to Germany, remember that you'll need a converter. Germany, like all of Europe, has a 220-volt electrical system, different from the 110 volt system in North America.

Clothing and Jewelry

Whether you are shopping for new clothes or just folding up the laundry, the following clothing vocabulary will come in handy.

CLOTHING (*DIE KLEIDUNG*)

bathing suit .... *der Badeanzug*
                dare BAH deh ahn tsook
boot.................... *der Stiefel*
                dare SHTEE fell
coat .... *der Mantel*
                dare MUHN tell
jacket .... *die Jacke*
                dee JUCK eh
jeans .... *die Jeans*
                dee jeans

pajamas	*der Schlafanzug*
	dare SHLAHF ahn tsook
pants	*die Hose*
	dee HOE zeh
raincoat	*der Regenmantel*
	dare RAY ghen muhn tell
sandals	*die Sandalen*
	dee ZAHN dah len
shoes	*die Schuhe*
	dee SHOO eh
shorts	*die kurze Hose/Shorts*
	dee KOORTS eh HOE zeh/shorts
sneakers	*die Turnschuhe*
	dee TOORN shoo eh
socks	*die Socken*
	dee ZAWK en
ski jacket	*die Skijacke*
	dee SHEE yuck eh
sweater	*der Pullover*
	dare pool OH vuh
T-shirt	*das T-Shirt*
	duss TEE shirt

Essential

Perhaps you noticed that *Hose* in German is a singular, whereas in English, "pants" is plural. If *Hose* is the subject of a sentence, its verb will be singular: *Diese Hose ist zu klein.* (These pants are too small.)

EN'S CLOTHING (*FRAUENKLEIDUNG*)

bikini ....*der Bikini*

dare bee KEE nee

blouse ....*die Bluse*

dee BLOO zeh

brassiere ....*der Büstenhalter*

dare BUE sten hult uh

dress ....*das Kleid*

duss klite

(half) slip ....*der Unterrock*

dare OON tuh rawk

high-heeled

shoes...................*die hochhackigen Schuhe*

dee HOECH huck ee ghen SHOO eh

miniskirt...............*der Minirock*

dare MINN ee rawk

nightgown ....*das Nachthemd*

duss NAHCHT hemt

panties.................*der Schlüpfer*

dare SHLUEP fuh

pantyhose, tights.....*die Strumpfhose*

dee SHTROOMPF hoe zeh

skirt ....*der Rock*

dare rawk

suit ....*das Kostüm*

duss kawss TUEM

stockings ....*die Strümpfe*

dee SHTRUEM pfeh

ⓔ *Essential*

Just as English uses "bra" for "brassiere," German also has an abbreviation for *der Büstenhalter: der BH* (dare BAY hah).

MEN'S CLOTHING (*MÄNNERKLEIDUNG*)

bow tie ....*die Fliege*
                    dee FLEE gheh

boxer shorts ....*die Boxershorts*
                    dee BAWX uh shorts

cummerbund.........*der Kummerbund*
                    dare KOOM uh boont

shirt ....*das Hemd*
                    duss hemt

sport jacket ....*der Sakko*
                    dare ZUK oh

suit ....*der Anzug*
                    dare AHN tsook

tie......................*der Schlips*
                    dare shlips

tuxedo.................*der Smoking*
                    dare SMOKE ing

undershirt.............*das Unterhemd*
                    duss OON tuh hemt

underwear ....*die Unterwäsche*
                    dee OON tuh vesh eh

ELRY (*DER SCHMUCK*)

rette .... *die Haarspange*
      dee HAHR shpung eh

bracelet .... *das Armband*
      duss AHRM bunt

brooch .... *die Brosche*
      dee BRAWSH eh

charm bracelet .... *das Armband mit Anhängern*
      duss AHRM bunt mit AHN heng uhn

cufflink .... *der Manschettenknopf*
      dare mahn SHETT en knawpf

earring .... *der Ohrring*
      dare ORE ring

engagement ring ..... *der Verlobungsring*
      dare fare LOE boongs ring

necklace .... *die Halskette*
      dee HULSS keh teh

pendant .... *der Anhänger*
      dare AHN heng uh

pin .... *die Anstecknadel*
      dee AHN shteck nah dell

ring .... *der Ring*
      dare ring

tie clasp .... *der Krawattenhalter*
      dare krah WAH ten hult uh

wedding ring .... *der Ehering*
      dare AY eh ring

ACCESSORIES (*DAS ACCESSOIRE*)

backpack..............*der Rucksack*	
	dare ROOK zuck
belt.....................*der Gürtel*	
	dare GUER tell
briefcase ....*die Aktentasche*	
	dee AHK ten tush eh
eyeglasses.............*die Brille*	
	dee BRILL eh
gloves.................*die Handschuhe*	
	dee HUNT shoo eh
handkerchief ....*das Taschentuch*	
	duss TUSH en tooch
hat.....................*der Hut*	
	dare hoot
mittens................*die Fausthandschuhe*	
	dee FOWST hunt shoo eh
muffler, scarf..........*der Schal*	
	dare shahl
purse...................*die Handtasche*	
	dee HUNT tush eh
ribbon ....*das Band*	
	duss bunt
neckscarf ....*das Halstuch*	
	duss HULLS tooch
shawl...................*das Schultertuch*	
	duss SHOOL tuh tooch

sses ....*die Sonnenbrille*
                    dee ZAWN en brill eh

 brella...............*der Regenschirm*
                    dare RAY ghen shirm

wallet ....*die Brieftasche*
                    dee BREEF tush eh

Colors and Sizes

Since colors are adjectives, refer to Chapter 2 for a review of how adjective endings work in German.

Fact

Since this book is mainly for speaking purposes, only the predicate adjective form of the German colors is provided.

COLORS (*FARBEN*)

purple.................*lila/violett*
                    LEE lah/vee oh LET

blue ....*blau*
                    blow (rhymes with "wow")

green...................*grün*
                    gruen

yellow.................*gelb*
                    ghelp

orange.................*orange*
                    oh RAWN zhe

red	*rot*
	rote
black	*schwarz*
	shvahrtz
white	*weiß*
	vice
grey	*grau*
	grow
brown	*braun*
	brown
pink	*rosa*
	ROH zah
light blue	*hellblau*
	HELL blow
dark blue	*dunkelblau*
	DOONK ell blow

SIZES (*DIE GRÖSSEN*)

clothing size	*die Kleidergröße*
	dee KLY duh grer seh
shoe size	*die Schuhgröße*
	dee SHOO grer seh

What size do you wear? I wear size . . .
Welche Größe tragen Sie? Ich trage Größe . . .
VELL cheh GRER seh TRAH ghen zee;
eech TRAH gheh grer seh . . .

Since German clothing and shoe sizes are numbered according to a different system than the British and

American system, you'll need to find a chart of equivalents. If you try something on that doesn't fit, the following vocabulary will come in handy.

USEFUL EXPRESSIONS

large .... *groß*
          groess
larger.................... *größer*
          GRERE suh
medium .... *mittelgroß*
          MIT ell groess
small.................... *klein*
          kline
smaller................. *kleiner*
          KLINE uh

Chapter 9
Activities and Entertainment

You've done a little shopping, found some new things to buy, and even got a haircut. Now you're ready to go out on the town and do some exploring or have some fun. You can take in a movie or a play, or perhaps go hear a concert. But in order to do these things, you'll need some vocabulary to see you through.

Verbs When You're a Participant

If you're involved in an activity, you're one of the participants. Let's look at the verbs *machen* (to do/make) and *spielen* (to play), which will be helpful when you're involved in an activity.

The Verb Machen

Present/Past

ich	*mache* [MAHCH eh]
	machte [MAHCH teh]
du.....................	*machst* [mahchst]
	machtest [MAHCH test]
er, sie, es.............	*macht* [mahcht]
	machte [MAHCH teh]
wir....................	*machen* [MAHCH en]
	machten [MAHCH ten]
ihr....................	*macht* [mahcht]
	machtet [MAHCH tet]
Sie	*machen* [MAHCH en]
	machten [MAHCH ten]
sie	*machen* [MAHCH en]
	machten [MAHCH ten]

What are you doing?
Was machen Sie?
vuss MAHCH en zee

I'm making the bed.
Ich mache das Bett.
eech MAHCH eh duss bet

The verb *machen* is used in many idiomatic expressions that cannot be translated word for word into English. Such expressions must simply be learned and used when appropriate. Let's look at a few useful examples.

Make yourself comfortable/at home.
Mach es dir gemütlich!
mahch ess deer gheh MUET lich

Hurry up.
Mach schnell!
mahch shnell

Never mind. It doesn't matter.
Macht nichts!
mahcht nihchtz

The Verb Spielen

Present/Past

ich	*spiele* [SHPEEL eh]
	spielte [SHPEEL teh]
du	*spielst* [shpeelst]
	spieltest [SHPEEL test]

sie, es	*spielt* [shpeelt]
	spielte [SHPEEL teh]
wir	*spielen* [SHPEEL en]
	spielten [SHPEEL ten]
ihr	*spielt* [shpeelt]
	spieltet [SHPEEL tet]
Sie	*spielen* [SHPEEL en]
	spielten [SHPEEL ten]
sie	*spielen* [SHPEEL en]
	spielten [SHPEEL ten]

The verb *spielen* is used very much like its English equivalent "to play:" You play sports, games, and musical instruments. And just like English, German doesn't need any prepositions following this verb. The sports, games, and instruments are all direct objects.

Do you play tennis?
Spielen Sie Tennis?
SHPEEL en zee TEN iss

We're playing chess.
Wir spielen Schach.
veer SHPEEL en shuch

My daughter plays piano.
Meine Tochter spielt Klavier.
MINE eh TAWCH tuh shpeel KLUH vee uh

Ⓔ *Essential*

Notice that, just like English, German doesn't always require a definite article with the name of a sport, game, or musical instrument: *Mein Sohn spielt Geige*. (My son plays [the] violin.)

Verbs When You're a Spectator

When you're just sitting back and taking in what others are doing, you're a spectator and not a participant. Two important verbs that allow you to be a spectator are *sehen* (to see) and *hören* (to hear).

The Verb Sehen

Present/Past

ich	*sehe* [ZAY eh]
	sah [zah]
du	*siehst* [zeest]
	sahst [zahst]
er, sie, es	*sieht* [zeet]
	sah [zah]
wir	*sehen* [ZAY en]
	sahen [ZAH en]
ihr	*seht* [zate]
	saht [zaht]
Sie	*sehen* [ZAY en]
	sahen [ZAH en]

sie .... *sehen* [ZAY en]
                     sahen [ZAH en]

I saw the children playing in the yard.
Ich sah die Kinder im Garten spielen.
eech zah dee KINN duh im GAHR ten SHPEEL en

She sees a pretty bird.
Sie sieht einen schönen Vogel.
zee zeet INE en SHERN en FOE ghel

Essential

In some special phrases the verb *sehen* can have a different meaning in English: *Ich sehe fern.* (I'm watching TV.) *Sieh mal!* (Look!)

The Verb Hören

Present/Past

ich .... *höre* [HER eh]
                     hörte [HER teh]
du .... *hörst* [herst]
                     hörtest [HER test]
er, sie, es .... *hört* [hert]
                     hörte [HER teh]
wir .... *hören* [HER en]
                     hörten [HER ten]

ihr	*hört* [hert]
	hörtet [HER tet]
Sie	*hören* [HER en]
	hörten [HER ten]
sie	*hören* [HER en]
	hörten [HER ten]

We hear the children singing.
Wir hören die Kinder singen.
veer HER en dee KINN duh ZING en

Do you hear the beautiful music?
Hören Sie die schöne Musik?
HER en zee dee SHERN eh moo ZEEK

Ⓔ *Essential*

In some special phrases the verb *hören* can have a different meaning in English: *Ich höre Radio.* (I'm listening to the radio.) *Lass mal etwas von dir hören!* (Keep in touch.)

Sports and Games

You can use the verb *spielen* when talking about the following sports and games.

SPORTS AND GAMES VOCABULARY

baseball	*der Baseball*
	dare BASE bul

basketball . . . . *der Basketball/Korbball*
dare BASS ket bul/KAWRP bul

cards . . . . *Karten*
KAHR ten

chess . . . . *der Schach*
dare shuch

golf . . . . *der Golf*
dare gawlf

hockey . . . . *der Hockey*
dare HAWK ee

soccer . . . . *der Fußball*
dare FOOSS bul

tennis . . . . *der Tennis*
dare TEN iss

volleyball . . . . *der Volleyball*
dare VAWL ee bul

Alert!

Notice that *Fußball* means "football" in British English but in American English it's "soccer." The Germans call American football *der amerikanische Football*.

The verb *gehen* (to go) is used when participating in a variety of other sports and activities.

	Present	Past
ich	*gehe* [GAY eh]	*ging* [ghing]
du	*gehst* [gayst]	*gingst* [ghingst]

er, sie, es	*geht* [GATE]	*ging* [ghing]
wir	*gehen* [GAY en]	*gingen* [GHING en]
ihr	*geht* [gate]	*gingt* [ghingt]
Sie	*gehen* [GAY en]	*gingen* [GHING en]
sie	*gehen* [GAY en]	*gingen* [GHING en]

Are you going biking?
Gehst du radfahren?
gayst doo RAHT fahr en

No, I'm going for a walk.
Nein, ich gehe spazieren.
nine eech GAY eh SHPUH tseer en

USEFUL VERBS

to go for a stroll .... *bummeln*
BOOM eln

to hike .... *wandern*
VUN dairn

to jog .... *joggen*
JAW ghen

to rollerskate .... *Rollschuh laufen*
RAWL shoo low fen

to row .... *rudern*
ROO dairn

to sail .... *segeln*
ZAY gheln

to ski .... *Ski laufen*
shee LOW fen

to surf . . . . *surfen*
ZOOR fen
to swim . . . . *schwimmen*
SHVIM en
to water ski . . . . *Wasserski laufen*
VUSS uh shee low fen

Hobbies

Besides sports and games, there are other hobbies you might be involved in. The following vocabulary will be helpful when you speak about hobbies with someone.

HOBBY VOCABULARY

cooking/to cook . . . . . *das Kochen/kochen*
duss KAWCH en
dancing/to dance . . . . *das Tanzen/tanzen*
duss TAHNTS en
fishing/to fish . . . . *das Angeln/angeln*
duss AHNG eln
to go fishing . . . . *fischen gehen/angeln gehen*
FISH en GAY en/AHNG eln GAY en
gardening . . . . *die Gartenarbeit*
dee GAHR ten ahr bite
to garden . . . . *im Garten arbeiten*
im GAHR ten AHR bite en
hunting/to hunt . . . . *die Jagd/jagen*
dee YAHKT/ YAH ghen
music . . . . *die Musik*
dee moo ZEEK

to listen to music ..... *Musik hören*
moo ZEEK HER en

to play music .... *Musik spielen*
moo ZEEK SHPEEL en

flute .... *die Flöte*
dee FLER teh

guitar .... *die Gitarre*
dee GHEE tahr eh

organ .... *die Orgel*
dee AWR ghel

piano.................. *das Klavier*
duss KLAH veer

trumpet............... *die Trompete*
dee TROME pay teh

violin.................. *die Geige*
dee GYE gheh

reading/to read....... *das Lesen/lesen*
duss LAY zen

Movies and Television

Other ways of enjoying a variety of entertainment types are at the movies or watching television. Here's some useful vocabulary for these venues.

MOVIE AND TELEVISION VOCABULARY

movie.................. *der Film*
dare film

feature film............ *der Spielfilm*
dare SHPEEL film

to watch a movie.....*sich einen Film ansehen*
zeech INE en film AHN zay en

movie theater.........*das Kino*
duss KEE noe

showing ....*die Vorstellung/Vorführung*
dee FORE shtell oong/
FORE fuer oong

seat.....................*der Platz*
dare plutz

television..............*das Fernsehen*
duss FAIRN zay en

to watch
television..............*fernsehen*
FAIRN zay en

television show.......*die Fernsehsendung*
dee FAIRN zay zen doong

dubbed................*synchronisiert*
zuen kroe nee ZEERT

subtitled ....*mit Untertiteln*
mit OON tuh tee teln

Essential

The verb *fernsehen* is used differently from its English equivalent "to watch television." The prefix *fern-* is placed at the end of the sentence and the word "television" doesn't even appear in the sentence: *Wir sehen jeden Abend fern.* (We watch television every evening.) *Siehst du schon wieder fern?* (Are you watching television again?)

Going to the Theater

There are many fine theaters throughout the German speaking world. Use the following vocabulary for live performances.

THEATER VOCABULARY

theater	*das Theater*
	duss TAY ah tuh
opera	*die Oper*
	dee OH puh
symphony	*die Sinfonie*
	dee zeen foe NEE
concert	*das Konzert*
	duss KONE tsairt
ballet	*das Ballett*
	duss buh LET
show/	
performance	*die Aufführung/Vorstellung*
	dee OW fuer oong/FORE shtell oong
balcony	*der Balkon*
	dare buhl KONE
box	*die Loge*
	dee LOE zheh
orchestra	*das Orchester*
	duss ore KESS tuh

Chapter 10
German for Business

Knowing some German business vocabulary can come in handy, particularly if you plan to work in Germany or deal with people who do. This chapter will provide you with words and phrases about professions, work situations, office equipment, banking, changing money, and school.

Jobs and Professions

Most nouns that describe professions have a masculine and feminine form that are identical except for the feminine *–in* ending, for example *der Lehrer/die Lehrerin* (teacher). Where the masculine and feminine in the following lists are identical, the feminine will be identified by the ending *–in*. If the feminine form is different from the masculine, the entire word will be provided for you.

PROFESSIONS (*BERUFE*)

actor .... *der Schauspieler/die –in*
　　　　　　　　　　dare SHAU shpeel uh/dee in

artist .... *der Künstler/die –in*
　　　　　　　　　　dare KUENST luh/dee in

baker.................... *der Bäcker/die –in*
　　　　　　　　　　dare BECK un/dee in

butcher .... *der Fleischer/die –in*
　　　　　　　　　　dare FLY shuh/dee in

carpenter.............. *der Tischler/die –in*
　　　　　　　　　　dare TISH luh/dee in

civil servant........... *der Beamte/die Beamtin*
　　　　　　　　　　dare bay UHM teh/dee bay UM tin

cook .... *der Koch/die Köchin*
　　　　　　　　　　dare kawch/dee KERCH in

dentist .... *der Zahnarzt/die Zahnärztin*
　　　　　　　　　　dare TSAHN ahrtst/dee TSAHN-
　　　　　　　　　　airts tin

doctor.................. *der Arzt/die Ärztin*
　　　　　　　　　　dare ahrtst/dee AIRTS tin

doorman ....*der Pförtner/die –in*
dare PFERT nuh/dee in

electrician.............*der Elektriker/die –in*
dare ay LECK tree kuh/dee in

employee..............*der/die Angestellte*
dare/dee AHN gheh shtell teh

engineer...............*der Ingenieur/die –in*
dare een zheh NEUR/dee in

fireman ....*der Feuerwehrmann/*
die Feuerwehrfrau
dare FOY uh vare mun/
dee FOY uh vare frow

lawyer/attorney.......*der Rechtsanwalt/*
die Rechtsanwältin
dare REHCHTS ahn vahlt/
dee REHCHTS ahn velt in

maid ....*das Dienstmädchen*
duss DEENST mate chen

manager...............*der Manager/die –in*
dare MEN uh juh/die in

mechanic ....*der Mechaniker/die –in*
dare may CHAHN ee kuh/dee in

nurse...................*die Krankenschwester*
dee KRUNK en shvess tuh

pharmacist............*der Apotheker/die –in*
dare AH poe tay kuh/dee in

plumber ....*der Klempner/die –in*
dare KLEMP nuh/dee in

police officer ....*der Polizist/die –in*
dare po lee TSIST/dee in

professor .... *der Professor/die –in*
dare pro FESS or/dee in
receptionist .... *der Empfangschef/*
(hotel) *die Empfangsdame*
dare emp FUNGS sheff/
dee emp FUNGS dah meh
secretary.............. *der Sekretär/die –in*
dare zeh kray TARE/dee in
student.................. *der Student/die –in*
dare shtoo DENT/dee in
waiter/server.......... *der Kellner/die –in*
dare KELL nuh/dee in
writer .... *der Schriftsteller/die –in*
dare SHRIFT shtell uh/dee in

Fact

Germans make a distinction between students in
early grades and students at the university level.
Pre-college pupils are called *Schüler* and *Schülerin*.
University level students are called *Student* and
Studentin.

German in the Workplace

To get along in the German workplace, you need
some basic vocabulary that deals with people in
various positions, employment, and earnings.

WORKPLACE VOCABULARY

boss	*der Chef/die –in*
	dare sheff/dee in
business card	*die Geschäftskarte*
	dee gheh SHEFTS kahr teh
CEO	*der Generaldirektor/die –in*
	dare ghen air AHL dee RECK tor/dee in
company	*die Firma*
	dee FEER mah
contract	*der Vertrag*
	dare fare TRAHK
interview	*das Vorstellungsgespräch*
	duss FORE shtell oongs
	gheh SHPRAYCH
job	*der Job*
	dare jawp
meeting	*das Treffen*
	duss TREFF en
minimum wage	*der Mindestlohn*
	dare MIN dest lone
raise	*die Lohnerhöhung*
	dee LONE air her oong
résumé	*der Lebenslauf*
	dare LAY bens lowf
salary, wages	*der Lohn*
	dare lone
employment	*die Arbeit*
	dee AHR bite
unemployed	*arbeitslos*
	AHR bites loes

to apply for a job ..... *sich bei einer Firma bewerben*
zeech by INE uh FEAR muh
beh VARE ben

to hire .... *einstellen*
INE shtell en

to fire .... *entlassen*
ent LUSS en

to lay off .... *vorübergehend entlassen*
fore UEB uh gay ent ent LUSS en

On the Phone

Speaking on the phone in a foreign language is a daunting experience. Not being able to see the person you're speaking to seems to make comprehension that much more difficult. Just do your best. When someone answers the phone, he or she is most likely to say *hallo* (hah LOE). But many answer with a last name such as Keller ("Keller speaking"). The following phrases will help you through your calls.

May I speak to . . . ?
Kann ich . . . sprechen?
kahn eech SHPREHCH en

I'd like to speak to . . .
Ich möchte . . . sprechen.
eech MERCH teh SHPREHCH en

Who is calling? This is . . .
Wer ruft an? Hier spricht . . .
vare rooft ahn heeuh shpricht

Don't hang up.
Bleiben Sie am Apparat!
BLY ben zee ahm ahp ah RAHT

I'll connect you.
Ich verbinde Sie.
eech fare BIN deh zee

The line is busy.
Die Leitung ist besetzt.
dee LYE toong ist beh ZEHTZT

TELEPHONE VOCABULARY

phone number	*die Telefonnummer*
	dee tay lay fone NOO muh
phone number	
prefix, area code.....	*die Vorwahl*
	dee FORE vahl
phone book...........	*das Telefonbuch*
	duss tay lay fone BOOCH
cell phone.............	*das Mobiltelefon/Handy*
	duss moe beel tay lay FONE/HEN dee
dial tone...............	*der Wählton*
	dare VALE tone
collect call	*das R-Gespräch*
	duss AIR gheh shpraych
local call	*das Ortsgespräch*
	duss OHRTS gheh shpraych
long distance call	*das Ferngespräch*
	duss FAIRN gheh shpraych

answering machine	*der Anrufbeantworter*
	dare AHN roof beh ahnt vawr tuh
to call	*anrufen/telefonieren*
	AHN roof fen/tay lay foe NEER en
to call back	*wieder anrufen*
	VEE duh AHN roof en
to be cut off	*unterbrochen werden*
	oont uh BRAWCH en VARE den
to dial a number	*eine Nummer wählen*
	INE eh NOO muh VAY len
to hang up	*aufhängen*
	OWF heng en
leave a message	*eine Nachricht hinterlassen*
	INE eh NAHCH richt HIN tuh luss en
to pick up the phone	*den Hörer abnehmen*
	dane HER uh AHP nay men
to ring	*klingeln*
	KLING eln

Essential

When completing a telephone call, you cannot use the expression *auf Wiedersehen* to say goodbye. Instead, say *auf Wiederhören*, which is something like "until I hear from you again."

Office Supplies and Equipment

You won't get any work done if you don't have the right supplies and equipment. Use the following German vocabulary to equip your office.

OFFICE VOCABULARY

desk	*der Schreibtisch*
	dare SHRIPE tish
inbox	*der Posteingang*
	dare PAWST ine gung
put in the outbox	*in die Post legen*
	in dee PAWST LAY ghen
(fountain) pen	*der Füller*
	dare FUE luh
pencil	*der Bleistift*
	dare BLY shtift
highlighter	*der Textmarker*
	dare TEXT mahr kuh
stapler	*der Hefter*
	dare HEFF tuh
staple	*die Heftklammer*
	dee HEFT klum uh
paper clip	*die Büroklammer*
	dee bue ROE klum uh
paper	*das Papier*
	duss puh PEER
piece of paper	*das Stück Papier*
	duss shtueck puh PEER
filing cabinet	*der Aktenschrank*
	dare AHK ten shrunk

file folder .... *die Mappe*
dee MUP eh

computer .... *der Computer*
dare kawm PYOO tuh

printer .... *der Drucker*
dare DROO kuh

copy machine .... *das Kopiergerät*
duss koe PEER gheh rate

fax machine .... *das Faxgerät*
duss FEX gheh rate

typewriter .... *die Schreibmaschine*
dee SHRIPE muh shee neh

calculator .... *der Rechner*
dare REHCH nuh

telephone .... *das Telefon*
duss tay lay FONE

e-mail .... *die E-Mail*
dee EE male

ⓔ *Fact*

Just having equipment in your office isn't enough.
You have to know how to use it. The German verb
"to use" is *benutzen* (beh NOOTZ en). The verb
"repair" is *reparieren* (ray pahr EER en). "To turn on"
and "to turn off" are *anschalten* (AHN shul ten) and
abschalten (AHP shul ten) respectively.

Banking and Changing Money

Money is important in everyday life and no less significant when traveling. Therefore, it's essential to know the vocabulary that will help you indicate your preferred method of payment, to change money, and to deal with bank accounts.

BANKING VOCABULARY

money	*das Geld*
	duss ghelt
bill, note, paper	
money	*der Geldschein*
	dare GHELT shine
cash	*das Bargeld*
	duss BAHR ghelt
change	*das Kleingeld*
	duss KLINE ghelt
coin	*die Münze*
	dee MUEN tseh
check	*der Scheck*
	dare sheck
checkbook	*das Scheckbuch*
	duss SHECK booch
certified check	*der bestätigte Scheck*
	dare beh SHTATE ick tuh sheck
traveler's check	*der Reisescheck*
	dare RYE zeh sheck
bank card/	
ATM card	*Die Bankkarte*
	dee BUNK kahr teh

credit card ....*die Kreditkarte*
dee kray DEET kahr the

bank ....*die Bank*
dee bunk

savings bank..........*die Sparkasse*
dee SHPAHR kuss eh

ATM/cash...................*der Geldautomat*
dispenser   dare GHELT ow toe maht

checking account....*das Girokonto*
duss GHEE roe kawn toe

savings account ......*das Sparkonto*
duss SHPAHR kawn toe

balance................*der Kontostand*
dare KAWN toe shtunt

bank statement.......*der Kontoauszug*
dare KAWN toe ows tsook

exchange rate ....*der Wechselkurs*
dare VEX ell koors

fee......................*die Gebühr*
dee gheh BUER

interest rate ....*der Zinssatz*
dare TSINZ zutz

loan ....*das Darlehen*
duss DAHR lay en

receipt ....*die Quittung*
dee KVIT oong

sum/total ....*die Summe/der Betrag*
dee ZOOM eh/dare beh TRAHK

yield....................*der Ertrag*
dare air TRAHK

ⓔ *Question?*

Are there other places besides a bank where I can change money?

There are usually money exchange offices at border crossings, large railroad stations, and airports. They're usually open beyond the regular hours of banks and savings banks, which is generally weekdays from 8:00 A.M. to 12:30 P.M. and then from 2:30 P.M. until 4:00 P.M. When looking for money exchange offices, watch for signs that say *Wechselstube* (VEX ell shtoo beh) or *Geldwechsel* (GHELT vex ell).

BANKING VERBS

to buy	*kaufen*
	KOW fen
to cash a check	*einen Scheck einlösen*
	INE en sheck INE ler zen
to change money	
(into euros)	*Geld (in Euro) wechseln*
	ghelt in OY roe VEX eln
to count	*zählen*
	TSAY len
to make a deposit	*einzahlen*
	INE tsah len
to earn	*verdienen*
	fair deen en
to need	*brauchen*
	BROW chen
to pay	*bezahlen*

beh TSAH len

to save money .... *Geld sparen*

ghelt SHPAH ren

to sell .... *verkaufen*

fare KOW fen

to sign.................. *unterschreiben*

oon tuh SHRIBE en

to spend .... *ausgeben*

OWS gay ben

to write a check ...... *einen Scheck schreiben*

INE en sheck SHRY ben

to withdraw
(from an account) ...*(von einem Konto) abheben*

fawn INE em KAWN toe AHP hay ben

In School

If you plan on taking some classes or are dealing with
someone who is, you'll find the following vocabulary
related to schools useful.

EDUCATION VOCABULARY

school .... *die Schule*

dee SHOO leh

elementary school ... die Grundschule

dee GROONT shoo leh

high school/
prep school .... *das Gymnasium*

duss ghuem NAHZ ee oom

college/university .... *die Universität*

dee oo nee vare see TATE

backpack.............*der Rucksack*
dare ROOK zahk

binder.................*die Ringmappe*
dee RING mup eh

book ....*das Buch*
duss BOOCH

chalk...................*die Kreide*
dee KRY deh

chalkboard ....*die Wandtafel*
dee VAHNT tah fell

classroom.............*das Klassenzimmer*
duss KLUSS en tsim uh

course/subject........*das Fach*
duss fahch

department ....*die Fakultät*
dee fah kool TATE

dictionary.............*das Wörterbuch*
duss VER tuh booch

eraser.................*der Radiergummi*
dare rah DEER goo mee

grade/year in
school ....*die Klasse*
dee KLUSS eh

grade/mark ....*die Note*
dee NOE teh

homework ....*die Schularbeit, die Hausaufgaben*
dee SHOOL ahr bite,
dee HOUSE owf gah ben

kindergarten..........*der Kindergarten*
dare KIN duh gahr ten

laptop.................*der Laptop/tragbare PC*
dare LEP tope/TRAHG bah re pay tsay

major subject.........*das Hauptfach*
duss HOWPT fahch

map....................*die Landkarte*
dee LUNT kahr teh

notebook..............*das Heft*
duss heft

paper.................*das Papier*
duss pah PEER

piece of paper........*das Stück Papier*
duss shtueck pah PEER

student desk..........*der Tisch*
dare tish

test/exam..............*das Examen*
duss ex AH men

general diploma......*der Schulabschluss*
dare SHOOL ahp shloos

prep school
diploma...............*das Abitur*
duss ah bee TOOR

to enroll (at a
university).............*immatrikulieren*
im mah tree koo LEER en

to work on a
doctorate..............*promovieren*
proe moe VEER en

to qualify as a university
lecturer .... *habilitieren*
                        hah bee lee TEER en
doctorate .... *der Doktorgrad*
                        dare DAWK tawr graht

Ⓔ Fact

The German school system does not parallel the American system. In fact, there are often significant differences from state to state within Germany. However, in general German children can find themselves in a nursery school, *kindergarten*, a form of elementary school, a form of middle school, and a form of high school. Be careful with the vocabulary. The German word *Hochschule* (HOECH shoo leh) looks like it relates to "high school," but it refers to college or university level education.

Chapter 11
German Medical Phrases

In case you need to go to a doctor or dentist or find a police station while traveling, these German words and phrases that deal with illness, medicine, and emergencies will come in handy.

Common Ailments

This German vocabulary deals with common ailments. These phrases can help you get the proper medical assistance when needed. The following vocabulary goes with *haben* (to have). For example, "to have arthritis" is *Arthritis haben*.

MEDICAL VOCABULARY WITH *HABEN*

arthritis . . . . *Arthritis*
ahrt REE tees

a cold . . . . *eine Erkältung*
INE eh air KELL toong

diarrhea . . . . *Durchfall*
DOORCH fuhl

an earache . . . . *Ohrenschmerzen*
OH rehn shmairtz en

a fever . . . . *ein Fieber*
ine FEE buh

the flu . . . . *die Grippe*
dee GRIP pch

frostbite . . . . *Erfrierungen*
air FREER oong en

hay fever . . . . *Heuschnupfen*
HOY shnoop fen

a headache . . . . *Kopfschmerzen*
KAWPF shmairtz en

heartburn . . . . *das Sodbrennen*
duss ZOHT brenn en

hemorrhoids . . . . *Hämorrhoiden*
hay more HOY den

seasickness ....*die Seekrankheit*
dee ZAY krunk hite
a runny nose..........*eine laufende Nase*
INE eh LOW fehn deh NAH zeh
sinusitis................*Sinusitis*
zee noo ZEE tees
a stomachache ....*Magenschmerzen*
MAH ghen shmairtz en

Another group of illnesses is expressed using the verb *sein* (to be). For example, "to be asthmatic" is *Asthmatiker sein.*

MEDICAL VOCABULARY WITH *SEIN*

asthmatic..............*Asthmatiker/asthmatisch*
AHST mah tee kuh/AHST mah tish
(have) a cold ....*erkältet*
air KELL tet
diabetic................*Diabetiker/diabetisch*
dee ah BATE ee kuh/
dee ah BATE ish
car sick ....*autokrank*
OW toe krunk

There is one term that is unique. If you wish to say you are an insomniac, use the phrase "*Ich leide an Schlaflosigkeit.*" (eech LYE deh ahn SHLAHF loze ik kite).

MEDICAL VERBS

to need an inhaler
einen Inhalationsapparat brauchen
INE en in hah lah tsee OWNS ahp ah raht BROW chen

to need sugar now
Zucker sofort brauchen
TSOO kuh zoe FORT BROW chen

to have high blood pressure
hohen Blutdruck haben
HOE en BLOOT drook HAH ben

to have low blood pressure
niedrigen Blutdruck haben
NEE dree ghen BLOOT drook HAH ben

to break one's arm, leg
sich den Arm/das Bein brechen
zeech dane ahrm/duss bine BREHCH en

 Alert!

Unlike English, German doesn't use possessive adjectives with parts of the body, such as "my arm" or "her leg." Instead, reflexive pronouns are used and the body part is preceded by a definite article (*der, die, das*): *Er bricht sich den Finger.* (He breaks his finger.)

Parts of the Body

Whether you are in a doctor's office or a clothing store, knowing the parts of the body is useful.

PARTS OF THE BODY (*KÖRPERTEILE*)

hair.....................*das Haar*

duss hahr

head ....*der Kopf*

dare kawpf

face ....*das Gesicht*

duss gheh ZIHCHT

eye ....*das Auge*

duss OW gheh

eyes ....*die Augen*

dee OW ghen

nose....................*die Nase*

dee NAH zeh

cheek ....*die Backe/Wange*

dee BUCK eh/VUNG eh

mouth ....*der Mund*

dare moont

lip ....*die Lippe*

dee LIP eh

tooth ....*der Zahn*

dare tsahn

ear......................*das Ohr*

duss ore

neck....................*der Hals*

dare huhls

chest	*die Brust*
	dee broost
stomach	*der Magen*
	dare MAH ghen
arm	*der Arm*
	dare ahrm
shoulder	*die Schulter*
	dee SHOOL tuh
elbow	*der Ellbogen*
	dare ELL boe ghen
wrist	*das Handgelenk*
	duss HUNT gheh lenk
hand	*die Hand*
	dee hunt
finger	*der Finger*
	dare FEENG uh
fingernail	*der Fingernagel*
	dare FEENG uh nah ghel
thumb	*der Daumen*
	dare DOW men
back	*der Rücken*
	dare RUE ken
leg	*das Bein*
	duss bine
knee	*das Knie*
	duss knee
ankle	*das Fußgelenk*
	duss FOOS gheh lenk

foot.....................*der Fuß*
dare foos

toe......................*der Zeh*
dare tsay

 **Essential**

> The words *Backe* and *Wange* tend to be used with the cheeks of the face. If you wish to refer to the "cheek" of the buttocks, you should use the term *die Hinterbacke* (dee HIN tuh buck uh).

Going to the Doctor

If you need to go the doctor while traveling, use the following vocabulary along with the common ailments already presented to describe your symptoms.

I'm cold. (I feel cold.)
Mir ist kalt.
meer ist kult.

I'm hot. (I feel hot.)
Mir ist heiß.
meer ist hice

He's dizzy. (He feels dizzy.)
Ihm ist schwindlig.
eem ist SHVIND lik

I'm jet lagged.
Mir macht die Zeitumstellung zu schaffen.
meer mahcht dee TSITE oom shtell oong tsoo SHUFF en

Ⓔ *Fact*

In some expressions, German uses the dative case to show how someone feels. Where English says "I feel hot," German says "to me it is hot" (*Mir ist heiß*.) Check Chapter 2 for a review of the dative case.

You can use the verb *sein* (to be) with many adjectives that express how you feel.

I am . . .
Ich bin . . .
eech bin

ICH BIN . . .

seasick	*seekrank*	
	ZAY krunk	
pregnant	*schwanger*	
	SHVUNG uh	
sick	*krank*	
	krunk	
tired	*müde*	
	MUE deh	

I'm constipated.
Ich leide an Verstopfung.
eech LYE deh ahn fare SHTAWP foong

He's sunburned.
Er hat einen Sonnenbrand.
air haht INE en ZAWN en brahnt

You can use the following phrase if you have an allergy:

I'm allergic to . . .
Ich bin gegen . . . allergisch.
eech bin GAY ghen . . . ull AIR gish

ICH BIN GEGEN . . . ALLERGISCH.

aspirin	*Aspirin*	
	ah spee REEN	
iodine	*Jod*	
	yote	
penicillin	*Penizillin*	
	pay nee tsee LEEN	

Essential

Review Chapter 7 if you are allergic to foods. You can also say that you're allergic to something by using the phrase *Ich bin Allergiker.* (I'm an allergy sufferer.)

SYMPTOMATIC VERBS

ache.....................*weh tun*	
	vay toon
to bleed................*bluten*	
	BLOO ten
to faint ....*in Ohnmacht fallen*	
	in OWN mahcht FUHL en
to fall....................*fallen*	
	FUHL en
to limp ....*hinken*	
	HINK en
to sneeze ....*niesen*	
	NEEZ en
to throw up ....*sich erbrechen*	
	zeech air BREHCH en

Going to the Dentist

Should you need to see a dentist while traveling, you want to be sure you can communicate your problems. Here is some essential German vocabulary that will be helpful.

DENTAL VOCABULARY

at the dentist's
office....................*beim Zahnarzt*
　　　　　　　　　　bime TSAHN ahrtst
tooth ....*der Zahn*
　　　　　　　　　　dare tsahn
baby tooth ....*der Milchzahn*
　　　　　　　　　　dare MIHLCH tsahn

back tooth ....*der Backenzahn ganz hinten*
dare BAHK en tsahn gahnts HIN ten

canine tooth ....*der Eckzahn*
dare ECK tsahn

front tooth.............*der vordere Zahn*
dare FORE dare eh tsahn

lower tooth............*der untere Zahn*
dare OON tare eh tsahn

molar ....*der Backenzahn*
dare BUCK en tsahn

upper tooth ....*der obere Zahn*
dare OH bare eh tsahn

wisdom tooth.........*der Weisheitszahn*
dare VICE hites tsahn

gums...................*das Zahnfleisch*
duss TSAHN flysh

jaw ....*der Kiefer*
dare KEE fuh

mouth ....*der Mund*
dare moont

abscess................*der Abszess*
dare ahp TSESS

toothache ....*das Zahnweh*
duss TSAHN vay

local anesthesia......*die örtliche Betäubung*
dee ERT lich eh beh TOY boong

a broken tooth........*ein abgebrochener Zahn*
ine AHP gheh brawch en uh tsahn

cavity ....*das Loch*
duss lawch

crown...................*die Zahnkrone*
dee TSAHN kroe neh

filling...................*die Zahnfüllung*
dee TSAHN fuell oong

infected................*infiziert*
in fee TSEERT

injection...............*die Injektion/Spritze*
dee in yeck tsee OWN/SHPRITZ eh

anesthetic.............*das Betäubungsmittel*
duss beh TOY boongs mit tell

open your mouth ....*machen Sie den Mund auf*
MAHCH en zee dane moont owf

root canal.............*die Wurzelbehandlung*
dee VOOR tsell beh hahnd loong

teeth cleaning........*die Zahnreinigung*
dee TSAHN rine ee goong

dental floss............*die Zahnseide*
dee TSAHN zye deh

toothbrush ....*die Zahnbürste*
dee TSAHN buers teh

false teeth.............*die Zahnprothese*
dee TSAHN pro tay zeh

A FEW DENTAL VERBS

to bleed................*bluten*
BLOOT en

to brush
(one's teeth) ....*sich die Zähne putzen*
zeech dee TSAY neh POOTZ en

to injure	*verletzen*
	FARE letz en
to lose	*verlieren*
	FARE lee ren
to pull out,	
extract	*extrahieren, ausziehen*
	ex trah HEE ren, OWS tsee en
to replace	*ersetzen*
	air ZETZ en
to rinse	*ausspülen*
	OWS shpue len

Ⓔ *Fact*

The German preposition *bei* is translated as "by" or "at" in English. It is also translated as "at a person's home, at someone's office," or "for a certain employer." For example, *bei Frau Keller* (at Mrs. Keller's house), *beim Arzt* (at the doctor's office), and *bei einer Bank arbeiten* (to work for a bank).

Going to the Pharmacy

The following list of words and phrases will come in handy when you pay a visit to a pharmacy.

PHARMACY VOCABULARY

pharmacy	*die Apotheke*
	dee ah poe TAY keh

pharmacist............*der Apotheker/die Apothekerin*
dare ah poe TAY kuh/
dee ah poe TAY kuh rin

antibiotics.............*das Antibiotikum*
duss ahn tee bee OH tee koom

antiseptic..............*das Antiseptikum*
duss ahn tee ZEP tee koom

aspirin ....*das Aspirin*
duss ah spee REEN

cough drop ....*das Hustenbonbon*
duss HOOS ten bawn bawn

cough syrup ....*der Hustensaft*
dare HOOS ten zuft

laxative................*das Abführmittel*
duss AHP fuer mit tell

medicine ....*das Medikament*
duss made ee kah MENT

pill......................*die Pille*
dee PILL eh

prescription...........*das Rezept*
duss ray TSEPT

remedy ....*das Heilmittel*
duss HILE mit tell

tablet (of
medicine) ....*die Tablette*
dee tah BLETT eh

mild....................*mild/leicht*
millt/lycht

strong..................*stark*
shtahrk

Emergencies and Disasters

You never know what could happen. Just to be on the safe side, here are some words and phrases that would be useful should you ever encounter an emergency.

EMERGENCY VOCABULARY

Emergency!	*Notfall!*
	NOTE fuhl
Fire!	*Feuer!*
	FOY uh
Police!	*Polizei!*
	poe lee TSY
Thief!	*Dieb!*
	deep
Watch out!	*Vorsicht!*
	FORE zihcht
accident	*der Unfall*
	dare OON fuhl
attack	*der Angriff*
	dare AHN griff
burglary	*der Einbruch/Diebstahl*
	dare INE brooch/DEEP shtahl
crash	*das Unglück, der Zusammenstoß*
	duss OON glueck,
	dare tsoo ZAHM en shtohs
explosion	*die Explosion*
	dee ex ploe zee OWN
fire	*das Feuer*
	duss FOY uh

fist fight .... *die Schlägerei*
dee shlay gare EYE

flood .... *die Überschwemmung*
dee ueb uh SHVEMM oong

gunshot .... *der Schuss*
dare shoos

mugging .... *der Straßenraub*
dare SHTRAHS en rowp

rape .... *die Vergewaltigung*
dee fare gheh VULL tee goong

to look for .... *suchen*
ZOO chen

ambulance .... *der Krankenwagen*
dare KRUNK en vah ghen

doctor .... *der Arzt/die Ärztin*
dare ahrtzt/dee AIRTZ tin

fire fighter .... *der Feuerwehrmann/*
die Feuerwehrfrau
dare FOY uh vare munn/
dee FOY uh vare frow

help .... *die Hilfe*
dee HILL feh

police officer .... *der Polizist/die Polizistin*
dare poe lee TSIST/dee poe lee TSIS tin

to drown .... *ertrinken*
air TRINK en

to be in labor .... *die Wehen bekommen*
dee VAY en beh KAWM en

to be wounded .... *verwundet sein*
fare VOON det zine

Chapter 12
In Your Community

In the previous chapters, you encountered German phrases that are helpful when traveling, dining out, going shopping, and even finding medical or dental care. This chapter will introduce you to vocabulary that deals with everyday tasks, such as grocery shopping, going to the post office, buying a newspaper, and a variety of other around-town activities.

At the Market

You can do your grocery shopping in Germany by going to the various specialty shops: a bakery, a butcher shop, a dairy store, and so on. Or you can make things more convenient for yourself by doing all your shopping in one place: the supermarket. Whichever you decide to do, the following phrases will come in handy.

USEFUL GROCERY SHOPPING TERMS

grocery store.......... *das Lebensmittelgeschäft*
duss LAY bens mit tell gheh sheft

outdoor market....... *der Markt*
dare mahrkt

supermarket .... *der Supermarkt*
dare ZOO puh mahrkt

this one................ *dieses*
DEE zess

that one................ *jenes*
YAY ness

these (ones) .... *diese*
DEE zeh

those (ones) .... *jene*
YAY neh

expensive .... *teuer*
TOY uh

cheap.................. *billig*
BILL ik

Fact

The demonstrative pronouns *dieser* and *jener* have to agree with the gender and number of the noun to which they refer. For example, since *Hut* (hat) is masculine, say *dieser Hut* and *jener Hut* (this hat, that hat). With a feminine noun such as *Lampe* (lamp), say *diese Lampe* and *jene Lampe* (this lamp, that lamp). With a neuter noun like *Buch* (book), say *dieses Buch* and *jenes Buch* (this book, that book). Plurals like *Schuhe* (shoes) become *diese Schuhe* and *jene Schuhe* (these shoes, those shoes).

Quantities, Weights, and Measures

It's important to be familiar with the German vocabulary that deals with quantities, in order to make purchases in the amount you want.

How much does it weigh? It weighs . . . kilograms.
Wie viel wiegt es? Es wiegt . . . Kilo.
vee feel veekt es / es veekt . . . KEE loe

MEASUREMENT VOCABULARY

piece . . . . *ein Stück*
                        ine shtueck
box . . . . *eine Schachtel*
                        INE eh SHUCH tell
can . . . . *eine Dose*
                        INE eh DOE zeh

bottle	....	*eine Flasche*
		INE eh FLUSH eh
jar	....	*ein Glas*
		ine glahss
gram	....	*ein Gramm*
		ine grahm
kilogram	....	*ein Kilogramm*
		ine KEE loe grahm
pound	....	*ein Pfund*
		ine pfoont
liter	....	*ein Liter*
		ine LEE tuh
milliliter	....	*ein Milliliter*
		ine MILL ih lee tuh
tin	....	*eine Büchse*
		INE eh BUEX eh

Ⓔ *Fact*

The German word *Pfund* (pound) shouldn't be confused with the weight used in England and North America. It is a metric term that means "half a kilogram" or 500 grams.

USEFUL MEASUREMENT PHRASES

enough	....	*genug*
		gheh NOOK
a lot, many	....	*viel*
		feel

how many,	
how much	*wie viele/wie viel*
	vee FEE leh/vee feel
more	*mehr*
	mare
less, fewer	*weniger*
	VAY nee guh
a little	*ein bisschen*
	ine BISS chen
too much,	
too many	*zu viel/zu viele*
	tsoo feel/tsoo FEE leh
no more bread	*kein Brot mehr*
	kine brote mare

Alert!

When using quantities in German, you don't have to use the word "of" when stating the quantity, such as "a jar of jam." In German, that phrase is *ein Glas Marmalade*. And be sure to review the metric system before arriving in Europe, because inches and gallons aren't used there.

At the Bakery

When you see a sign with the word *Bäkerei* on it, you've found a store that primarily sells bread and rolls. A *Konditorei*, on the other hand, is a store that offers cookies, tarts, cakes, and fancy pastries. It often provides a little seating area where you can snack on a pastry and drink a cup of coffee or glass of wine. The following German vocabulary will be useful when you visit one of these stores.

BÄKEREI AND *KONDITOREI* VOCABULARY

baker....................*der Bäcker/die Bäckerin*
dare BECK uh/dee BECK uh rin

bakery..................*die Bäkerei*
dee BECK uh rye

pastry shop............*die Konditorei*
dee kawn dee toe RYE

bread....................*das Brot*
duss brote

rye bread...............*das Roggenbrot*
duss RAW ghen brote

whole wheat
bread....................*das Vollkornbrot*
duss FAWL kohrn brote

a loaf of black
bread....................*ein Laib Schwarzbrot*
ine lipe SHVAHRTS brote

doughnut...............*der Berliner*
dare BARE lee nuh

cake......................*der Kuchen*
dare KOOCH en

cookie..................*das Plätzchen*
duss PLETZ chen

roll.......................*das Brötchen*
duss BRERT chen

At the Post Office

The words *die Post* and *das Postamt* tell you that you are
at the post office.

POSTAL VOCABULARY

post office	*die Post/das Postamt*
	dee pawst/duss PAWST ahmt
mail	*die Post*
	dee pawst
mailbox	*der Briefkasten*
	dare BREEF kuss ten
postage	*das Porto*
	duss PORE toe
stamp	*die Briefmarke*
	dee BREEF mahr keh
book of stamps	*das Briefmarkenheft*
	duss BREEF mahr ken heft
air mail	*die Luftpost*
	dee LOOFT pawst
zip code	*die Postleitzahl*
	dee PAWST lite tsahl
change of address	*die Adressenänderung*
	dee ah DRESS en end uh roong
express mail	*der Eilbrief*
	dare ILE breef
general delivery	*postlagernd*
	PAWST lah gairnt
insured	*versichert*
	fare ZICH airt

receipt .... *die Quittung*
dee KVIT oong

registered .... *eingeschrieben*
INE gheh shree ben

postcard............... *die Postkarte*
dee PAWST kahr teh

special delivery ...... *die Eilzustellung*
dee ILE tsoo shtell oong

address .... *die Adresse/Anschrift*
dee ah DRESS eh/AHN shrift

envelope .... *der Briefumschlag*
dare BREEF oom shlahk

letter .... *der Brief*
dare breef

package .... *das Paket*
duss pah KATE

recipient............... *der Empfänger/die Empfängerin*
dare emp FENG uh/
dee emp FENG uh rin

sender .... *der Absender/die Absenderin*
dare AHP zen duh/
dee AHP zen duh rin

size..................... *die Größe*
dee GRER seh

weight .... *das Gewicht*
duss gheh VICHT

money order.......... *die Postanweisung*
dee PAWST ahn vye zoong

postage due........... *die Nachgebühr*
dee NAHCH gheh buer

🄴 Alert!

If you want to mail letters and postcards when you're out on the street, look for a yellow box. That's the traditional color for the German postal system.

Computers and Cybercafés

If you don't have your computer along on your trip, a good place to check e-mails, print documents, or just surf the net is the cybercafé.

TECHNOLOGY VOCABULARY

computer..............	*der Computer*
	dare kawm PYOO tuh
cybercafé	*das Cybercafé*
	duss SYE buh kah fay
CD-ROM drive........	*das CD-ROM-Laufwerk*
	duss tsay day rome LOWF vairk
e-mail..................	*die E-Mail*
	dee EE mail
e-mail address........	*die E-Mail-Adresse*
	dee ee mail ah DRESS eh
file......................	*die Datei*
	dee dah TYE
hard drive.............	*das Festplattenlaufwerk*
	duss FEST plutt en lowf vairk
Internet	*das Internet*
	duss IN tuh net

keyboard .... *die Tastatur*
dee tahs tah TOOR

laptop .... *der Laptop*
dare LEP tawp

monitor .... *der Monitor, Bildschirm*
dare MAWN ee toh, BILT sheerm

mouse .... *die Maus*
dee mouse

per hour .... *pro Stunde*
proe SHTOON deh

printer .... *der Drucker*
dare DROOK uh

software .... *die Software*
dee SAWFT ware

hardware .... *die Hardware*
dee HARD ware

website .... *die Website*
dee WEB site

to download .... *herunterladen*
hare OON tuh lah den

receive .... *empfangen*
emp FAHNG en

send .... *senden*
ZEN den

to click on .... *anklicken*
AHN klick en

to delete .... *löschen*
LER shen

Chapter 13
Miscellaneous German

The categories of vocabulary in this chapter are not interconnected, but they play an important role in the German language. It will be helpful to be familiar with them. You'll encounter words and phrases that deal with weather, physical descriptions, personality, moods, and a little romance.

Weather Words

The weather is always a topic of conversation whether in English or German, so you'll find the following vocabulary useful.

How's the weather? It is . . .
Wie ist das Wetter? Es ist . . .
vee ist duss VET tuh ess ist

WEATHER VOCABULARY

hot.....................*heiß*
hice

cold ....*kalt*
kult

cool ....*kühl*
kuehl

warm ....*warm*
vahrm

nice...................*schön*
shern

bad.....................*schlecht*
shlehcht

humid.................*feucht*
foycht

rainy ....*regnerisch*
RAYG nuh rish

sunny ....*sonnig*
ZAWN ik

cloudy ....*bewölkt*
beh VERLKT

stormy .... *stürmisch*
SHTUER mish

windy .... *windig*
VIN dik

foggy .... *neblig*
NAY blik

The names of the seasons are nouns, so they are always capitalized in German.

SEASONS OF THE YEAR (*DIE JAHRESZEITEN*)

spring .... *Frühling/Frühjahr*
FRUEH ling/FRUEH yahr

summer .... *Sommer*
ZAW muh

autumn .... *Herbst*
hairpst

winter .... *Winter*
VINN tuh

 Fact

Some weather expressions require the use of a verb instead of an adjective, for example: *Es regnet.* (It's raining.) *Es schneit.* (It's snowing.) *Es donnert.* (It's thundering.) *Es blitzt.* (Lightning is flashing.) *Es gießt in Strömen.* (It's raining cats and dogs.)

Descriptive Data

If you want to describe the new person you're dating or tell the police about a pickpocket you saw, you'll need some descriptive vocabulary.

DESCRIPTIVE VOCABULARY

man	*der Mann*
	dare munn
woman	*die Frau*
	dee frow
boy	*der Junge*
	dare YOONG eh
girl	*das Mädchen*
	duss MATE chen
tall	*groß*
	grohss
short	*kurz*
	koortz
fat	*dick*
	dick
thin	*dünn*
	duenn
handsome/	
beautiful	*hübsch*
	huebsh
ugly	*hässlich*
	HESS lich
tan	*sonnengebräunt*
	ZAWN en gheh broynt

pretty .... *schön*
shern

eyes .... *die Augen*
dee OW ghen

hair.................... *das Haar*
duss hahr

freckles .... *die Sommersprossen*
dee ZAWM uh shpraws en

dimples............... *die Grübchen*
dee GRUEP chen

wrinkles .... *die Falten*
dee FUL ten

Personality Traits

If you want to describe someone's personality traits rather than physical traits, you need a different kind of vocabulary. Here are some helpful words.

USEFUL DESCRIPTIVE ADJECTIVES

athletic .... *atlethisch/sportlich*
aht LAY tish/SHPAWRT lich

boring .... *langweilig*
LUNG vye lik

brave.................... *tapfer*
TAHPF uh

conceited .... *eingebildet*
INE gheh bill det

cowardly .... *feige*
FYE gheh

forgetful	*vergesslich*
	fare GHESS lich
friendly	*freundlich*
	FROYNT lich
funny	*komisch*
	KOE mish
generous	*großzügig*
	GROHS tsueg ik
hardworking	*fleißig*
	FLY sik
impatient	*ungeduldig*
	OON gheh dool dik
interesting	*interessant*
	in tare eh SAHNT
kind	*nett*
	net
likeable	*sympathisch*
	zuem PAH tish
lazy	*faul*
	fowl
mean	*gemein*
	gheh MINE
naïve	*naiv*
	nah EEF
open-minded	*aufgeschlossen*
	OWF gheh shlaws en
outgoing	*kontaktfreudig*
	kawn TAHKT froy dik
patient	*geduldig*
	gheh DOOL dik

patriotic	*patriotisch*
	pah tree OH tish
playful	*scherzhaft*
	SHAIRTZ huft
reserved	*zurückhaltend*
	tsoo RUEK hult ent
serious	*ernst*
	airnst
shy	*schüchtern*
	SHUECH tuhn
smart	*klug*
	klook
sophisticated	*kultiviert*
	kool tee VEERT
strong	*stark*
	shtahrk
studious	*lerneifrig*
	LAIRN ife rik
stupid	*dumm*
	doom
weak	*schwach*
	shvuhch

Mood Management

Use the following German vocabulary to describe some-one's mood.

angry	*böse*
	BER zeh

annoying .... *ärgerlich*
AIR guh lich

ashamed .... *beschämt*
beh SHAYMT

calm .... *ruhig*
ROO ik

confident.............. *zuversichtlich*
TSOO fare zihcht lich

confused .... *verwirrt*
fare VEERT

disappointed .... *enttäuscht*
ent TOYSHT

embarrassed.......... *verlegen*
fare LAY ghen

excited................. *aufgeregt*
OWF gheh raykt

exhausted............. *erschöpft*
air SHERPFT

happy.................. *froh*
froe

hyper(active) .... *aufgedreht*
OWF gheh drayt

lonely .... *einsam*
INE zum

nervous................ *nervös*
nare VERSE

sad .... *traurig*
TROW rik

sloppy.................. *schlampig*
SHLUMP ik

tired....................*müde*
                    MUE deh
worried................*besorgt*
                    beh ZAWRGT

Ⓔ *Alert!*

Some descriptions in German have to be made by using a verbal expression rather than an adjective, for example: *Ich habe Angst.* (I'm scared.) *Es tut mir Leid.* (I'm sorry.)

The Language of Romance

German is not one of the Romance languages, but still it has a wealth of expressions that have to do with dating, love, and marriage.

I love you, too.
Ich liebe dich auch.
eech LEE beh deech owch

Do you want to marry me?
Willst du mich heiraten?
villst doo meech HYE rah ten

ROMANTIC VOCABULARY

to date ....*(mit jemandem) ausgehen*
                    mitt YAY mahn dem OWS gay en

to get engaged..............	*sich (mit jemandem) verloben*
	zeech mitt YAY mahn dem
	fare LOE ben
to get married	*heiraten*
	HYE rah ten
engagement	*die Verlobung*
	dee fare LOE boong
wedding.....................	*die Hochzeit*
	dee HOECH tsite
wedding anniversary......	*der Hochzeitstag*
	dare HOECH tsites tuck
honeymoon.................	*die Flitterwochen*
	dee FLIT uh vawch en
present	*das Geschenk*
	duss gheh SHENK
flowers......................	*die Blumen*
	dee BLOO men
candy........................	*die Süßigkeiten*
	dee ZUESS ik kite en
perfume	*das Parfüm*
	duss pahr FUEM
jewelry......................	*der Schmuck*
	dare shmook
engagement ring...........	*der Verlobungsring*
	dare fare LOE boogs ring
wedding ring	*der Ehering*
	dare AYE eh ring
bride	*die Braut*
	dee browt

groom	*der Bräutigam*
	dare BROY tee gahm
husband, spouse...........	*der Mann/Gatte*
	dare munn/GUT teh
fiancé, fiancée..............	*der/die Verlobte*
	dare/dee fare LOEP teh
lover..........................	*der/die Geliebte*
	dare/dee gheh LEEP teh
boyfriend....................	*der Freund*
	dare froynt
wife, spouse	*die Frau/Gattin*
	dee frow/GUT tin
girlfriend	*die Freundin*
	dee FROYN din
friend, acquaintance..............	*der/die Bekannte*
	dare/dee beh KAHN teh

🅔 *Fact*

Germans make a clear distinction between a close friend and someone who is a casual friend or acquaintance. Call someone who is dear to you *Freund* or *Freundin*. But someone you just met or who is not very close to you is a *Bekannte*.

Chapter 14
Common German Expressions

In the previous chapters of this book, you encountered vocabulary that was organized by topic or situation. This final chapter is a little different. A series of commonly used German expressions will be presented for their special usage of certain verbs. Some of the expressions are highly idiomatic and can't always be translated literally into English, but in all cases their use will be fully explained.

Espressions with *Es Gibt*

The phrase *es gibt* is used where in English you say "there is" or "there are." *Es gibt* comes from the verb *geben* (to give). However, other special expressions that contain the verb *geben* exist that also don't conform to the general meaning "give."

 Fact

It is common in all languages to have combinations of words that, when translated into another language, make little or no sense. These are called idioms, and they require special attention.

THE VERB *GEBEN*

Present	Past
ich gebe [GAY beh]	*gab* [gahp]
du gibst [geepst]	*gabst* [gahpst]
er, sie, es gibt [geept]	*gab* [gahp]
wir geben [GAY ben]	*gaben* [GAH ben]
ihr gebt [gaybt]	*gabt* [gahpt]
Sie geben [GAY ben]	*gaben* [GAH ben]
sie geben [GAY ben]	*gaben* [GAH ben]

I don't believe it. (There's no such thing.)
Das gibt es ja gar nicht.
duss geept ess yah gahr nihcht

It happens all the time.
Das gibt es wohl häufiger.
duss geept ess vole HOY fee guh

It wasn't like that back in my day.
Zu meiner Zeit gab es das nicht.
tsoo MINE uh tsite gahp ess duss nihcht

Is there anything else?
Gibt es noch etwas?
geept ess nohch EHT wuss

There'll be rain tomorrow.
Morgen gibt es Regen.
MORE ghen geept ess RAY ghen

There's nothing to eat.
Es gibt nichts zu essen.
ess geebt nihchtz tsoo ESS en

What is there to drink?
Was gibt es zu trinken?
vuss geept ess tsoo TRINK en

What's new?
Was gibt es Neues?
vuss geept ess NOY ess

There's a new movie at the movie theater today.
Im Kino gibt es heute einen neuen Film.
im KEE noe geept ess HOY teh INE en NOY en film

EXPRESSIONS WITH *GEBEN*

to send off to be printed …	*zum Druck geben*
	tsoom drook GAY ben
to send out for repairs……	*zur Reparatur geben*
	tsoor ray pah rah TOOR
	GAY ben
to mail ……………………	*zur Post geben*
	tsoor pawst GAY ben
to kick ……………………	*einen Tritt geben*
	INE en tritt GAY ben
to talk nonsense…………	*Unsinn von sich geben*
	OON zin fawn zeech GAY ben

Alert!

Although *es gibt* is most often translated as "there is" or "there are," don't confuse that with the adverbs *da* and *dort* which mean "there" as a location.

Expressions with *Machen*

There are a variety of useful expressions that are formed from the verb *machen* (to make). The English translation of some of these special expressions does not make sense if you translate it literally.

Present	Past
ich mache [MAHCH eh]	*machte* [MAHCH teh]
du machst [mahchst]	*machtest* [MAHCH test]
er, sie, es macht [mahcht]	*machte* [MAHCH teh]
wir machen [MAHCH en]	*machten* [MAHCH ten]
ihr macht [mahcht]	*machtet* [MAHCH tet]
Sie machen [MAHCH en]	*machten* [MAHCH ten]
sie machen [MAHCH en]	*machten* [MAHCH ten]

This makes you thirsty.
Das macht Durst.
duss mahcht doorst

This makes you hungry.
Das macht Hunger.
duss mahcht HOONG uh

I take a picture.
Ich mache ein Foto.
eech MAHCH eh ine FOE toe

Make yourself comfortable.
Mach es dir gemütlich!
mahch ess deer gheh MUET lich
What should I do?
Was soll ich nur machen?
vuss zawl eech noor MAHCH en

EXPRESSIONS WITH *MACHEN*

to do one's hair.......*sich die Haare machen*
zeech dee HAH reh MAHCH en

to do one's
fingernails.............*sich die Fingernägel machen*
zeech dee FING uhr nay ghell
MAHCH en

to give a party ....*ein Fest machen*
ine fest MAHCH en

to take a course ......*einen Kurs machen*
INE en koors MAHCH en

to make enemies.....*sich Feinde machen*
zeech FINE deh MAHCH en

to get to work.........*sich an die Arbeit machen*
zeech ahn dee AHR bite MAHCH en

Fact

> The verb *machen* is most often translated as "to
> make." In some expressions it can also be translated
> as "to do." *Was machst du*? (What are you doing?)

Expressions with *Gehen*

The verb *gehen* is used to mean "to go" on foot. But it
occurs in other expressions where the meaning is sometimes varied.

THE VERB *GEHEN*

Present	**Past**
ich gehe [GAY eh]	*ging* [ging]
du gehst [gayst]	*gingst* [gingst]
er, sie, es geht [gate]	*ging* [ging]
wir gehen [GAY en]	*gingen* [GING en]
ihr geht [gate]	*gingt* [gingt]
Sie gehen [GAY en]	*gingen* [GING en]
sie gehen [GAY en]	*gingen* [GING en]

Yes, that will work.
Ja, das geht.
yah duss gate

This clock is wrong.
Diese Uhr geht falsch.
DEE zeh oor gate fulsh

That will be difficult.
Das wird schwer gehen.
duss vihrd shvare GAY en

How are you (formal)?
Wie geht es Ihnen?
vee gate ess EE nen

I'm fine, thanks.
Es geht mir gut, danke.
ess gate meer goot dunk eh

He only thinks of money.
Ihm geht es nur um Geld.
eem gate ess noor oom ghelt

EXPRESSIONS WITH *GEHEN*

to face the street	*nach der Straße gehen*
	nahch dare SHTRAH seh
	GAY en
to face north	*nach Norden gehen*
	nahch NORE den GAY en
to make a detour	*einen Umweg gehen*
	INE en OOM vake GAY en
to go into the movies	*ins Kino gehen*
	ins KEY no GAY en
to go to bed	*schlafen gehen*
	SHLAH fen GAY en
to go shopping	*einkaufen gehen*
	INE kow fen GAY en

Alert!

You can use *nach . . . gehen* with any number of expressions that say that something "faces" or "looks out on" a place. But *gehen* can also be used with the preposition *zu* and the prefix *hinaus* to achieve a similar meaning.

Expressions with *Lassen*

The basic meaning of *lassen* is "let" or "allow." However, it is frequently used to express that someone "gets" or "has" something done. In addition, there are some useful idiomatic expressions to know.

THE VERB *LASSEN*

Present	Past
ich lasse [LUSS eh]	*ließ* [lees]
du lässt [lest]	*ließt* [leest]
er, sie, es lässt [lest]	*ließ* [lees]
wir lassen [LUSS en]	*ließen* [LEES en]
ihr lasst [lusst]	*ließt* [leest]
Sie lassen [LUSS en]	*ließen* [LEES en]
sie lassen [LUSS en]	*ließen* [LEES en]

Let the boys enjoy themselves.
Lass den Jungen den Spaß!
luss dane YOONG en dane shpahs

I didn't let the stranger come into my apartment.
Ich ließ den Fremden nicht in meine Wohnung.
eech lees dane FREM den nihcht in MINE eh VOE noong

She gets the car repaired.
Sie lässt den Wagen reparieren.
zee lest dane VAH ghen ray pah REE ren

I got my suit dry-cleaned.
Ich ließ mir den Anzug reinigen.
eech lees meer dane AHN tsook RINE ih gen

EXPRESSIONS WITH *LASSEN*

to run water in the
bathtub . . . . *Wasser in die Wanne laufen lassen*
　　　　　　　　　VUSS uh in dee VUNN eh
　　　　　　　　　LOW fen LUSS en

to send one's
regards . . . . *grüßen lassen*
　　　　　　　　　GRUE sen LUSS en

to let know . . . . *wissen lassen*
　　　　　　　　　VISS en LUSS en

to leave in peace . . . . . *in Frieden lassen*
　　　　　　　　　in FREE den LUSS en

to leave alone . . . . *allein lassen*
　　　　　　　　　ah LINE LUSS en

Lassen is often used in an impersonal expression that
means "it can be . . . " In the present and past tenses, it is
stated as *es lässt sich* and *es ließ sich*.

The door can't be opened.
Die Tür lässt sich nicht öffnen.
dee tuer lest zeech nihcht ERF nen

That can be done.
Das lässt sich machen.
duss lest zeech MAHCH en

It couldn't be denied.
Es ließ sich nicht verleugnen.
ess lees zeech nihcht fare LOYG nen

That couldn't be proved.
Das ließ sich nicht beweisen.
duss lees zeech nihcht beh VIZE en

Expressions with *Tun*

The verb *tun* means "to do" and has a variety of uses with that meaning. However, it appears in special expressions where that meaning is often changed.

THE VERB *TUN*

Present	**Past**
ich tue [TOO eh]	*tat* [taht]
du tust [toost]	*tatst* [tahtst]
er, sie, es tut [toot]	*tat* [taht]
wir tun [toon]	*taten* [TAHT en]
ihr tut [toot]	*tatet* [TAHT et]
Sie tun [toon]	*taten* [TAHT en]
sie tun [toon]	*taten* [TAHT en]

What are you doing here?
Was tun Sie hier?
vuss toon zee heer

What should I do?
Was soll ich tun?
vuss zawl eech toon

There's nothing you can do about it.
Dagegen kannst du nichts tun.
dah GAY ghen kahnst doo nihchst toon

Go on!
Tu's doch!
toose dawch

I'm busy.
Ich habe zu tun.
eech HAH beh tsoo toon

Don't do this to me.
Tu mir das nicht an!
too meer duss nihcht ahn

She's got a heart problem.
Sie hat es mit dem Herzen zu tun.
zee haht ess mitt dame HARE tsen tsoo toon

EXPRESSIONS WITH *TUN*

to have its effect............	*seine Wirkung tun*
	ZINE eh VIRK oong toon
to do a favor	*einen Gefallen tun*
	INE en gheh FULL en toon

to put water in the pot..... *Wasser in den Topf tun*

                      VUSS uh in dane tawpf toon

to act as if . . . . *tun, als ob . . .*

                      toon ahls awp

The Modal Auxiliaries

The modal auxiliaries have an important function in the German language. They describe a person's attitude or obligation regarding an activity. The modals are: *dürfen* (may, be allowed), *können* (can, to be able to), *müssen* (must, to have to), *sollen* (should, ought to), and *wollen* (to want to).

Their present and past tense conjugations are:

THE VERB *DÜRFEN*

Present	Past
ich darf [dahrf]	*durfte* [DOORF teh]
du darfst [dahrfst]	*durftest* [DOORF test]
er, sie, es darf [dahrf]	*durfte* [DOORF teh]
wir dürfen [DUERF en]	*durften* [DOORF ten]
ihr dürft [duerft]	*durftet* [DOORF tet]
Sie dürfen [DUERF en]	*durften* [DOORF ten]
sie dürfen [DUERF en]	*durften* [DOORF ten]

THE VERB *KÖNNEN*

Present	Past
ich kann [kahn]	*konnte* [KAWN teh]
du kannst [kahnst]	*konntest* [KAWN test]

er, sie, es kann [kahn]	*konnte* [KAWN teh]
wir können [KERN en]	*konnten* [KAWN ten]
ihr könnt [kernt]	*konntet* [KAWN tet]
Sie können [KERN en]	*konnten* [KAWN ten]
sie können [KERN en]	*konnten* [KAWN ten]

THE VERB *MÜSSEN*

Present

Past

ich muss [moos]	*musste* [MOOS teh]
du musst [moosst]	*musstest* [MOOS test]
er, sie, es muss [moos]	*musste* [MOOS teh]
wir müssen [MUESS en]	*mussten* [MOOS ten]
ihr müsst [muesst]	*musstet* [MOOS tet]
Sie müssen [MUESS en]	*mussten* [MOOS ten]
sie müssen [MUESS en]	*mussten* [MOOS ten]

THE VERB *SOLLEN*

Present

Past

ich soll [zawl]	*sollte* [ZAWL teh]
du sollst [zawlst]	*solltest* [ZAWL test]
er, sie, es soll [zawl]	*sollte* [ZAWL teh]
wir sollen [ZAWL en]	*sollten* [ZAWL ten]
ihr sollt [zawlt]	*solltet* [ZAWL tet]
Sie sollen [ZAWL en]	*sollten* [ZAWL ten]
sie sollen [ZAWL en]	*sollten* [ZAWL ten]

THE VERB *WOLLEN*

Present	**Past**
ich will [vill]	*wollte* [VAWL teh]
du willst [villst]	*wolltest* [VAWL test]
er, sie, es will [vill]	*wollte* [VAWL teh]
wir wollen [VAWL en]	*wollten* [VAWL ten]
ihr wollt [vawlt]	*wolltet* [VAWL tet]
Sie wollen [VAWL en]	*wollten* [VAWL ten]
sie wollen [VAWL en]	*wollten* [VAWL ten]

Using Modal Auxiliaries

The modal auxiliaries are used together with another verb—an infinitive, for example *mitkommen*.

COMMON EXPRESSIONS

May I come
along?..................*Darf ich mitkommen?*
                 dahrf eech MIT kaw men

Can they come
along?..................*Können sie mitkommen?*
                 KERN en zee MIT kaw men

Do I have to come
along?..................*Muss ich mitkommen?*
                 moos eech MIT kaw men

Should he come
along?..................*Soll er mitkommen?*
                 zawl air MIT kaw men

Do you want to come
along?.................*Wollen Sie mikommen?*

VAWL en zee MIT kaw men

Ⓔ *Essential*

Notice that the infinitive in sentences with modals
appears at the end of the sentence. Any number
of infinitives can be used with each of the modal
auxiliaries.

We have to . . .
Wir müssen . . .
veer MUESS en

WIR MÜSSEN . . .

. . . drive to the city	. . . *in die Stadt fahren*
	in dee shtuht FAH ren
. . . go shopping	. . . *einkaufen gehen*
	INE kow fen GAY en
. . . find the money	. . . *das Geld finden*
	duss ghelt FIN den
. . . buy two airline tickets	. . . *zwei Flugtickets kaufen*
	tsvy FLOOK tick ets KOW fen

Do you want . . .
Willst du . . .
villst doo

COMMON GERMAN EXPRESSIONS

WILLST DU . . .

. . . to go to the movies?	. . . *ins Kino gehen?*
	ins KEE noe GAY en
. . . to go out for Mexican this evening?	
	. . . *heute abend mexikanisch essen?*
	HOY teh AH bent mex ee KAH nish ESS en

I can't . . .
Ich kann nicht . . .
eech kahn nihcht

ICH KANN NICHT . . .

. . . understand	. . . *verstehen*
	fare SHTAY en
. . . sleep	. . . *schlafen*
	SHLAH fen
. . . go to the theater	. . . *ins Theater gehen*
	ins tay AH tuh GAY en

Ⓔ *Question?*

How do I use the modal auxiliaries in the future tense?

As with all infinitives in future tense sentences, the modal auxiliary infinitive appears at the end of the sentence. But since modals are used with other infinitives, the future tense sentence will have two infinitives at the end. Present Tense: *Er kann es nicht verstehen.* (He can't understand it.) Future Tense: *Er wird es nicht verstehen können.* (He won't be able to understand it.)

The Special Case of Haben

A very important phrase is formed with the subjunctive of *haben* (to have). Its conjugational forms are *ich hätte, du hättest, er/sie/es hätte, wir hätten, ihr hättet, Sie hätten,* and *sie hätten.* It is used together with *sollen* to express regret at someone's actions: *Das hättest du nicht tun sollen.* (You shouldn't have done that.)

You shouldn't have . . .
Das hätten Sie nicht . . . sollen
duss HETT en zee nihcht . . . zawlen

DAS HÄTTEN SIE NICHT . . .

. . . said that	. . . *sagen sollen*
	ZAH ghen ZAWL en
. . . bought that	. . . *kaufen sollen*
	KOW fen ZAWL en
. . . written that	. . . *schreiben sollen*
	SHRY ben ZAWL en
. . . ordered that	. . . *bestellen sollen*
	beh SHTELL en ZAWL en
. . . asked that	. . . *fragen sollen*
	FRAH ghen ZAWL en
. . . broken that	. . . *kaputt machen sollen*
	kah POOT MAHCH en ZAWL en
. . . lost that	. . . *verlieren sollen*
	fare LEER en ZAWL en

Ⓔ *Alert!*

This kind of special phrase is really quite easy to use. Just don't forget that the sentence ends with two infinitives side-by-side: *Das hätte ich nicht essen sollen.* (I shouldn't have eaten that.)

Special Phrases and Word Order

In general, there are not many complications with German word order. One exception is the placement of an infinitive at the end of sentence that has a modal auxiliary. Many conjunctions also signal a word order change.

Using Dass *and* Ob

The conjunctions *dass* (that) and *ob* (whether/if) require the conjugated verb in the clause that follows them to be the last element. These conjunctions are used frequently with an important verb: *wissen* (to know). Here are this verb's present and past tense conjugations.

THE VERB *WISSEN*

Present	Past
ich weiß [vice]	*wusste* [VOOS teh]
du weißt [vysst]	*wusstest* [VOOS test]
er, sie, es weiß [vice]	*wusste* [VOOS teh]

wir wissen [VISS en]	*wussten* [VOOS ten]
ihr wisst [visst]	*wusstet* [VOOS tet]
Sie wissen [VISS en]	*wussten* [VOOS ten]
sie wissen [VISS en]	*wussten* [VOOS ten]

Ⓔ *Alert!*

Don't confuse *wissen* and *kennen*. They both mean "to know." However, *wissen* means having knowledge and *kennen* means being acquainted with someone, for example: *Ich weiß, wo er wohnt.* (I know where he lives.) *Ich kenne die junge Frau.* (I know the young woman.)

I know.
Ich weiß.
eech vice

I don't know.
Ich weiß (es) nicht.
ecch vice ess nihcht

As far as I know.
Soviel ich weiß.
zoe feel eech vice

You always know better.
Sie wissen immer alles besser.
zee VISS en IM muh ULL ess BESS uh

How should a person know that?
Woher soll man das wissen?
VOE hare zawl munn duss VISS en

You never know!
Man kann nie wissen.
munn kahn nee VISS en

I don't know anything about it.
Ich weiß von nichts.
eech vice fawn nihchts

WISSEN

to know

about ....*wissen von*

VISS en fawn

to know how to

behave..........................*sich zu benehmen wissen*

zeech tsoo beh NAME en VISS en

When *wissen* is used with the conjunctions *dass* and *ob*, the conjugated verb appears at the end of the sentence.

I know that . . .
Ich weiß, dass . . .
eech vice duss

ICH WEISS, DASS . . .

. . . the hotel isn't far from here
. . . *das Hotel nicht weit von hier entfernt ist*
duss HOE tell nihcht vite fawn heer ent FAIRNT ist

. . . his brother is well again
. . . *sein Bruder wieder gesund ist*
zine BROO duh VEE duh gheh ZOONT ist

. . . I need more money
. . . *ich mehr Geld brauche*
  eech mare ghelt BROW cheh

. . . she bought a blouse
. . . *sie eine Bluse kaufte*
zee INE eh BLOOZE eh KOWF the

Do you know whether (if) . . .
Wissen Sie, ob . . .
VISS en zee awp

WISSEN SIE, OB . . .

. . . the inn is still open?
. . . *der Gasthof noch offen ist?*
dare GAHST hofe nawch AW fen ist

. . . this street goes to city hall?
. . . *diese Straße zum Rathaus führt?*
DEEZ eh SHTRAH seh tsoom RAHT house fuert

. . . they have my luggage?
. . . *sie mein Gepäck haben?*
zee mine gheh PECK HAH ben

. . . service is included?
. . . *die Bedienung inbegriffen ist?*
dee beh DEEN oong in beh GRIFF en ist

You can even use interrogative words like *wann, wo,* and *wie* as conjunctions that require the same word order.

Do you know when the next train will arrive?
Weißt du, wann der nächste Zug kommt?
vysst doo vunn dare NAYX teh tsook kawmt

I don't know where Mr. Keller lives.
Ich weiß nicht, wo Herr Keller wohnt.
ecch vice nihcht voe hare KELL uh voent

Do you know how you get to the airport?
Wissen Sie, wie man zum Flughafen kommt?
VISS en zee vee munn tsoom FLOOK hah fen kawmt

Question?

How do I know when a verb will be the last element in a clause?

All conjunctions like *dass* and *ob* and interrogatives like *wann* and *wo* require the verb to be the last element in a clause. There are four exceptions to that rule: *aber* (but), *denn* (because), *oder* (or), and *und* (and).

Imperatives

Because there are three forms of "you" in German, there are three forms of the commands: one for *du*, one for *ihr*, and one for *Sie*.

Commands with Du

Most second person singular commands (*du*) are formed by dropping the *–en* ending from an infinitive. This is the imperative that is used with family members, friends, or children.

Infinitive	Imperative	English
kommen	*Komm!*	come
singen	*Sing!*	sing
fahren	*Fahr schneller!*	drive faster
machen	*Mach schnell!*	hurry up
spielen	*Spiel im Garten!*	play in the garden

Commands with Ihr

The pronoun *ihr* is the informal plural of *du*. Its imperative form is usually identical to its present tense conjugation.

Infinitive	Imperative	English
lachen	*Lacht nicht!*	Don't laugh!
singen	*Singt!*	Sing!
sprechen	*Sprecht Deutsch!*	Speak German!
bleiben	*Bleibt zu Hause!*	Stay at home!
besuchen	*Besucht Onkel Hans!*	Visit Uncle Hans!

Commands with Sie

The *Sie* form of the imperative is the formal form. In most cases, use the infinitive and place the pronoun *Sie* after it, and you will have the command form.

Infinitive	Imperative	English
sich setzen	*Setzen Sie sich!*	Sit down!
helfen	*Helfen Sie mir!*	Help me!
verkaufen	*Verkaufen Sie den Wagen!*	Sell the car!
aufhören	*Hören Sie auf!*	Stop that!
sein	*Seien Sie nicht böse!*	Don't be angry!

Fact

In public places where announcements are made, you will often hear an imperative given in the form of an infinitive. If you use this form with a person you're speaking with, it will sound a bit abrupt. It's used primarily to give information to large groups, for example: *Zurückbleiben*! (Stand back!) *Nicht Rauchen*! (No smoking!)

Appendix A
German-English Dictionary

The gender and number of the nouns listed here is indicated by *m.* for masculine, *f.* for feminine, *n.* for neuter, *sing.* for singular, and *pl.* for plural. Both German and English verbs are provided as infinitives.

Abend m.	evening	Angestellte m./f.	employee
Abendbrot n.	supper, dinner	Angriff m.	attack
Abendessen n.	supper, dinner	Angst haben	to be afraid
aber	but	Anhänger m.	pendant
abfertigen	to check in	anklicken	to click on
Abfertigungsschalter m.	check-in window	Ankunft f.	arrival
Abflug m.	departure (plane)	Anrufbeantworter m.	answering machine
Abführmittel n.	laxative	anrufen	to call, phone
abgeben	to hand in	anschalten	turn on
abheben	to withdraw (money)	Anschrift f.	mailing address
Abitur n.	prep school diploma	ansehen (sich)	to look at
abnehmen	to take off, take from	Ansichtskarte f.	picture postcard
Abreise f.	departure	Anstecknadel f.	decorative pin
abschalten	to turn off	Antibiotikum n.	antibiotic
Absender m.	sender	anziehen (sich)	to dress, put on
abstrakt	abstract	Anzug m.	suit
Abszess m.	abscess	Apfel m.	apple
acht	eight	Apfelsine f.	orange
achtzehn	eighteen	Apotheke f.	pharmacy, drugstore
achtzig	eighty	Apotheker/-in m./f.	pharmacist
Adresse f.	address	Apparat m.	apparatus, appliance
Affe m.	ape, monkey	Appetit m.	appetite
Afrikaner/-in m./f.	African person	Aprikose f.	apricot
Ägypter/-in m./f.	Egyptian person	April m.	April
Aktenschrank m.	file cabinet	Arbeit f.	work, job
Aktentasche f.	briefcase	arbeitslos	unemployed
aktiv	active	ärgerlich	annoyed
Akzent m.	accent	Arm m.	arm
alle	all, everyone	Armband n.	bracelet
allein	alone	Arthritis f.	arthritis
Allergie f.	allergy	Artischocke f.	artichoke
allergisch	allergic	Artist/-in m./f.	artist
alles	everything	Arzt/Ärztin m./f.	doctor, physician
als ob	as if	Aspirin n.	aspirin
alt	old	Asthmatiker/-in m./f.	asthmatic (person)
Amerika	America	asthmatisch	asthmatic
Amerikaner/-in m./f.	American person	athletisch	athletic
Änderung f.	change	attraktiv	attractive
angeln	to fish	auch	also, too

auf	on	*Bargeld n.*	cash
auf Wiederhören	goodbye (on phone)	*Baseball m.*	baseball
auf Wiedersehen	goodbye	*Basketball m.*	basketball
Aufführung f.	performance	*Beamte/Beamtin m./f.*	civil servant
aufgeben	to give up, check in	*bedeuten*	to mean
aufgedreht	hyperactive	*Bedienung f.*	service; call to a waiter
aufgeregt	excited	*bei*	by, at
aufgeschlossen	open-minded	*Bein n.*	leg
aufhängen	to hang up (phone)	*Bekannte m./f.*	acquaintance
aufhören	to stop, cease	*Bekleidungsgeschäft n.*	clothing store
aufmachen	to open	*belegt*	no vacancy
Auge n.	eye	*benehmen (sich)*	to behave
Augenzahn m.	eyetooth	*Benzin n.*	gasoline
August m.	August	*Berliner m.*	doughnut
aus	out, from	*Beruf m.*	occupation
ausgeben	to spend (money)	*beschämt*	ashamed
ausspülen	to rinse out	*beschleunigen*	to accelerate
Ausweis m.	identification	*besetzt*	occupied
ausziehen (sich)	to undress	*besorgt*	worried
Auto n.	automobile, car	*bestätigt*	certified
Autobahn f.	highway	*bestellen*	to order
Automatik-Getriebe n.	automatic transmission	*besuchen*	to visit
		Betäubung f.	anesthesia
Baby n.	baby	*Betrag m.*	total amount
Backe f.	cheek	*Bett n.*	bed
Backenzahn m.	molar	*beweisen*	to prove
Bäcker/-in m./f.	baker	*bewerben (sich)*	to apply for
Bäckerei f.	bakery	*bezahlen*	to pay, pay for
Badeanzug m.	swimsuit	*BH m.*	bra
Badewanne f.	bathtub	*Bier n.*	beer
Bahnhof m.	train station	*Bikini m.*	bikini
Bahnsteig m.	train platform	*Bildschirm m.*	screen, monitor
Balkon m.	balcony	*billig*	cheap, inexpensive
Ballett n.	ballet	*billion f.*	trillion
Banane f.	banana	*Birne f.*	pear
Band n.	ribbon	*bis*	until
Bank f.	bank	*bisschen*	little bit
bar	in cash	*bitte*	please
Bär m.	bear	*blau*	blue

Blaubeere f.	blueberry	*Brust f.*	chest
bleiben	to stay, remain	*Buch n.*	book
Bleichmittel n.	bleach	*Büchse f.*	tin
Bleistift m.	pencil	*Büroklammer f.*	paper clip
blind	blind	*bürsten*	to brush
Blinker m.	turn signal	*Büstenhalter m.*	brassiere
blitzen	to flash lightning	*bummeln*	to stroll
Blume f.	flower	*Bus m.*	bus
Blumenkohl m.	cauliflower	*Busbahnhof m.*	bus station
Bluse f.	blouse	*Bushaltestelle f.*	bus stop
Blutdruck m.	blood pressure	*Butter f.*	butter
bluten	to bleed	*Buttermilch f.*	buttermilk
Bohne f.	bean	*CD-ROM-Laufwerk n.*	CD-ROM drive
Boot n.	boat	*Chance f.*	chance
Bortkarte f.	boarding card	*Chef/-in m./f.*	boss
böse	angry, mad	*chemische Reinigung f.*	dry cleaner
Boxershorts pl.	boxer shorts	*Cocktail m.*	cocktail
Brasilianer/-in m./f.	Brazilian	*Computer m.*	computer
brauchen	to need	*Cousin m., Cousine f.*	cousin
braun	brown	*Cybercafé n.*	cybercafé
Braut f.	bride	*da*	there
Bräutigam m.	groom	*dagegen*	against it
brechen	to break	*danken*	to thank
Bremse f.	brake	*Darlehen n.*	loan
Bremslicht n.	brakelight	*das*	the (neuter), that
Brief m.	letter	*dass (conjunction)*	that
Briefkasten m.	mailbox	*Datei f.*	file
Briefmarke f.	stamp	*Dauerwelle f.*	permanent wave
Briefmarkenheft n.	book of stamps	*Daumen m.*	thumb
Brieftasche f.	wallet	*dein*	your (*du*)
Briefumschlag m.	envelope	*demokratisch*	democratic
Brille f.	eyeglasses	*denn*	because
Brombeere f.	blackberry	*der*	the (masculine)
Brosche f.	broach	*deutsch*	German
Brot n.	bread	*Deutsche m./f.*	German (person)
Brötchen n.	roll	*Deutschland*	Germany
Bruder m.	brother	*Dezember m.*	December
Brunnen m.	fountain, well	*Diabetiker/-in m./f.*	diabetic (person)

diabetisch	diabetic	*effektiv*	effectiv
Diät f.	diet	*Ehering m.*	wedding ring
dick	fat, thick	*Ei n.*	egg
die	the (feminine and plural)	*Eilbrief m*	express letter
Dieb m.	thief	*Eilzustellung f.*	express delivery
Diebstahl m.	theft	*ein, eine*	a, an
Dienstag m.	Tuesday	*einander*	one another, each other
Dienstmädchen n.	servant (girl)	*Einbahnstraße f.*	one-way street
dieser, diese, dieses	this	*einbiegen*	to turn
Diplomat m.	diplomat	*Einbruch m.*	burglary, break-in
doch	but, still	*eingebildet*	conceited
Doktorgrad m.	doctorate	*eingeschrieben*	registered
donnern	to thunder	*einkaufen*	to shop
Donnerstag m.	Thursday	*Einkaufszentrum n.*	shopping center
Doppelbett n.	double bed	*einlösen*	to cash (in)
dort	there	*einmal*	once
dort drüben	over there	*eins*	one
Dose f.	can	*einsam*	lonely
drei	three	*Einsamkeit f.*	loneliness
dreißig	thirty	*Einsteigekarte*	boarding card
dreizehn	thirteen	*einstellen*	to employ
Drogerie f.	drugstore	*einzahlen*	to deposit (money)
Druck m.	print, printing	*Eis n.*	ice; ice cream
Drucker m.	printer	*Elefant m.*	elephant
du	you (singular, informal)	*Elektriker m.*	electrician
dünn	thin	*elf*	eleven
dürfen	may, to be allowed	*Ellbogen m.*	elbow
dumm	stupid	*E-Mail f.*	e-mail
dunkelblau	dark blue	*E-Mail-Adresse f.*	e-mail address
durch	through	*empfangen*	to receive
Durchfall m.	diarrhea	*Empfänger/-in m./f.*	receiver, addressee
durchgebraten	well done (meat)	*Empfangschef m.*	receptionist (hotel)
durchspülen	to rinse	*Empfangsdame f.*	receptionist (hotel)
Durst m.	thirst	*England*	England
Dusche f.	shower	*Engländer/-in m./f.*	English person
duschen (sich)	to take a shower	*englisch gebraten*	rare (meat)
duzen	to say *du*	*englisch*	English
Eckzahn m.	canine tooth	*Enkel m.*	grandson
Economywagen m.	economy car	*Enkelin f.*	granddaughter

...fernt	away, remote	Falten pl.	wrinkles
...ntlassen	to release, fire	Familie f.	family
Entschuldigung f.	excuse	Familienname m.	surname
enttäuscht	disappointed	Farbe f.	color
er	he, it (masculine)	färben	to color, dye
erbrechen (sich)	to throw up	faul	lazy
Erbsen pl.	peas	Fausthandschuhe pl.	mittens
Erdbeere f.	strawberry	Faxgerät n.	fax machine
Erdgeschoss n.	ground floor	Februar m.	February
Erdnuss f.	peanut	feige	cowardly
Erfrierungen pl.	frostbite	Feind m.	enemy
erkälten (sich)	to catch a cold	Feld n.	field
Erkältung f.	cold (illness)	Fenster n.	window
erklären	to declare; explain	Ferngespräch n.	long-distance call
ernst	serious	Fernlicht n.	high beams
erschöpft	exhausted	Fernsehapparat m.	television set
ersetzen	to replace	fernsehen	to watch television
Ertrag m.	gain (financial)	Fernsehsendung f.	television program
ertrinken	to drown	Fest n.	celebration
es	it	Festplattenlaufwerk n.	hard drive
es gibt	there is/are	Fett n.	fat
essen	to eat	feucht	humid
Esszimmer n.	dining room	Feuer n.	fire
etwas	something	Feuerwehrmann m.	firefighter
euer	your (ihr)	Feuerwehrfrau f.	firefighter
Europäer/-in m./f.	European person	Fieber n.	fever
Examen n.	examination	Film m.	film, movie
Explosion f.	explosion	Filz m.	felt
extrahieren	to extract	finden	to find
Fach n.	subject	Finger m.	finger
fahren, fahren mit	to drive, to travel by	Fingernagel m.	fingernail
Fahrer m.	driver	Firma f.	company
Fahrrad n.	bicycle	Fisch m.	fish
Fahrstuhl m.	elevator	fischen	to fish
Fahrt f.	trip, drive	Fischgeschäft n.	fish market
fair	fair	Flasche f.	bottle
Fakultät f.	department (academic)	Fleisch n.	meat
fallen	to fall	Fleischer/-in m./f.	butcher
falsch	false, wrong	Fleischerei f.	butcher shop

fleißig	diligent	*fünfzehn*	fifteen
Fliege f.	bow tie; fly	*fünfzig*	fifty
fliegen	to fly	*für*	for
Flitterwochen pl.	honeymoon	*Fuß m.*	foot
Flöte f.	flute	*Fußball m.*	soccer
Flug m.	flight	*Fußgelenk n.*	ankle
Fluggast m.	airline passenger	*Gabel f.*	fork
Fluggesellschaft f.	airline	*Garage f.*	garage
Flughafen m.	airport	*Garten m.*	garden
Flugsteig m.	gate (airport)	*Gartenarbeit f.*	gardening
Flugticket n.	airline ticket	*Gärtner/-in m./f.*	gardener
Flugzeug n.	airplane	*Gas n.*	gas
Flur m.	hallway	*Gaspedal n.*	gas pedal
fönen	to blow dry	*Gasse f.*	lane
Foto n.	photo	*Gasthof m.*	inn
fragen	to ask	*Gatte m.*	spouse
Franzose/Französin m./f.	French person	*Gattin f.*	spouse
Frau f.	woman, wife	*geben*	to give
Frauenkleidung f.	women's clothing	*Gebühr f.*	fee
Freitag m.	Friday	*Gedeck-Karte f.*	fixed menu
Fremde m./f.	stranger	*geduldig*	patient
freuen (sich)	to be glad, happy	*Gefallen m.*	favor
Freund m.	friend, boyfriend	*Geflügel n.*	poultry
Freundin f.	friend, girlfriend	*gegen*	against
freundlich	kind	*gehen*	to go (on foot)
freundlich	friendly	*Geige f.*	violin
Frieden m.	peace	*gelb*	yellow
frisch	fresh	*Geld n.*	money
Frischkäse m.	cream cheese	*Geldautomat m.*	ATM
Friseur/-in m./f.	barber, hair stylist	*Geldschein m.*	bill, paper money
Frisur f.	hairdo	*Geldwechsel m.*	currency exchange
froh	happy	*Geliebte m./f.*	lover
Frosch m.	frog	*gemein*	mean, nasty
früh	early	*gemütlich*	cozy, comfotable
Frühling m.	spring	*Generaldirektor m.*	CEO
Frühstück n.	breakfast	*genug*	enough
führen	to lead	*Gepäck n.*	baggage
Füller m.	fountain pen	*Gepäckausgabe f.*	baggage claim
fünf	five	*geradeaus*	straight ahead

gern	gladly	*haben*	to have
gern haben	to like	*Hähnchen n.*	chicken
Geschäft n.	store	*halb*	half
Geschäftskarte f.	business card	*halb durchgebraten*	medium rare/
geschehen	to happen		well done (meat)
Geschenk n.	present, gift	*hallo*	hi
Geschwindikeitsbeschränkung f.	speed	*Hals m.*	neck
	limit	*Halskette f.*	necklace
Gesicht n.	face	*Halstuch n.*	scarf, neckscarf
gesund	healthy	*Hämorrhoiden pl.*	hemorrhoids
Gesundheit f.	health	*Hand f.*	hand
Getränk n.	beverage	*Handgelenk n.*	wrist
Gewicht n.	weight	*Handgepäck n.*	hand luggage
Gewitter n.	storm	*Handschuhe pl.*	gloves
gießen	to pour	*Handtasche f.*	handbag
Girokonto n.	checking account	*Handtuch n.*	towel
Gitarre f.	guitar	*Handy n.*	cell phone
Glas n.	glass, jar	*Hardware f.*	hardware (computer)
gleich	equal, same	*hart*	hard
Golf m.	golf	*hässlich*	ugly
Grab n.	grave	*häufig*	frequent, frequently
Gramm n.	gram	*Hauptfach n.*	major subject
grau	gray	*Hauptgericht n.*	main course
Grippe f.	flu	*Haus n.*	house
groß	big, tall	*Hausaufgaben f.*	homework
Größe f.	size	*Haustier n.*	pet
Großmutter f.	grandmother	*Heft n.*	notebook
Großvater m.	grandfather	*Hefter m.*	stapler
großzügig	generous	*Heftklammer f.*	staple
Grübchen n.	dimple	*Heidelbeere f.*	blueberry
grün	green	*Heilmittel n.*	remedy
Grundschule f.	elementary school	*Heimweh n.*	homesickness
grüßen	to greet	*heiraten*	to marry
Gürtel m.	belt	*heiß*	hot
Gurke f.	cucumber	*heißen*	to be called
gut	good, well	*heizen*	to heat
Gymnasium n.	prep school	*helfen*	to help
Haar n.	hair	*hellblau*	light blue
Haarspange f.	barrette	*Hemd n.*	shirt

Herbst m.	autumn
Hering m.	herring
Herr m.	Mr., sir
herunterladen	to download
Herz n.	heart
Heuschnupfen m.	hay fever
heute	today
Hilfe f.	help, aid
Himbeere f.	raspberry
hinken	to limp
hinlegen (sich)	to lie down
hinsetzen (sich)	to sit down
hinter	behind
hinterlassen	to leave behind
Hin-und-Rückflugkarte f.	round-trip airline ticket
historisch	historic
Hitze f.	heat
hoch	high
hochhackige Schuhe pl.	high-heel shoes
Hochschule f.	higher school (as in university)
Hochstuhl m.	highchair
Hochzeit f.	wedding
Hochzeitstag m.	anniversary
Hockey m.	hocky
holen	to get, fetch
hören	to hear
Hörer m.	receiver (phone)
Hose f.	pants
Hotel n.	hotel
hübsch	beautiful, handsome
Huhn n.	chicken
Hummer m.	lobster
hundert	hundred
Hunger m.	hunger
Hustenbonbon n.	cough drop
Hustensaft m.	cough syrup
Hut m.	hat

ich	I
ihr	you (plural, informal)
ihr	her, their
Ihr	your (Sie)
immatrikulieren	to matriculate
immer	always
inbegriffen	included
Inder/-in m./f.	(East) Indian person
Industrie f.	industry
infiziert	infected
Ingenieur/-in m./f.	engineer
Inhalationsapparat m.	inhaler
Injektion f.	injection, shot
innovativ	innovative
interessant	interesting
Internet n.	Internet
Italiener/-in m./f.	Italian person
italienisch	Italian
ja	yes
Jacke f.	jacket
Jagd f.	hunt
jagen	to hunt
Januar m.	January
Japaner/-in m./f.	Japanese person
Jeans pl.	jeans
jeder, jede, jedes	each
jemand	someone
jener, jene, jenes	that
Job m.	job
Jod n.	iodine
joggen	to jog
Joghurt m.	yogurt
Juli m.	July
Junge m.	boy
Juni m.	June
Kabrio n.	convertible
Kaffee m.	coffee
Kakao m.	cocoa
Kalb n.	calf

Kalbfleisch n.	veal
kalt	cold
Kanadier/-in m./f.	Canadian person
Kapitalist/-in m./f.	capitalist
kaputt	broken
Karotte f.	carrot
Karten pl.	cards
Kartoffel f.	potato
Käse m.	cheese
kaufen	to buy
Kaufhaus n.	department store
kein	no, not one
Keine Ursache	don't mention it
Keller m.	basement
Kellner/-in m./f.	waiter
kennen	to know, be acquainted
kennen lernen	to meet
Kette f.	chain
Kiefer m.	jaw
Kilo n.	kilogram
Kilogramm n.	kilogram
Kilometer m.	kilometer
Kind n.	child
Kindergarten m.	kindergarten
Kino n.	movie theater
Kirche f.	church
Kirsche f.	cherry
Kissen n.	pillow
Klampner/-in m./f.	plumber
Klasse f.	class, grade
Klassenzimmer n.	classroom
Klavier n.	piano
Kleid n.	dress
Kleidergröße f.	dress size
Kleiderschrank m.	wardrobe
klein	small, little
Kleingeld n.	change
Klimaanlage f.	air conditioning
klingeln	to ring

klug	smart, clever
Knabe m.	lad
Knecht m.	farmhand
Knie n.	knee
Koch/Köchin m./f.	cook, chef
kochen	to cook
komisch	funny
kommen	to come
kommunistisch	communist
Kompaktwagen m.	compact car
Konditorei f.	pastry shop
Konferenz f.	conference
können	can, to be able to
kontaktfreudig	outgoing
Kontoauszug m.	bank statement
Kontostand m.	bank balance
Konzert n.	concert
Kopf m.	head
Kopfsalat m.	lettuce
Kopfschmerzen pl.	headache
Kopiergerät n.	copy machine
Korbball m.	basketball
korrekt	correct
Korridor m.	corridor
kosten	to cost
krank	sick
Krankenhaus n.	hospital
Krankenschwester f.	nurse
Krankenwagen m.	ambulance
Krawattenhalter m.	tie clasp
Kreditkarte f.	credit card
Kreide f.	chalk
kritisch	critical
Küche f.	kitchen
kuh f.	cow
kühl	cool
Künstler/-in m./f.	artist
kultiviert	sophisticated
Kummerbund m.	cummerbund

Kursus m.	course
küssen	to kiss
kurz	short
lachen	to laugh
Laden m.	shop
Laib m.	loaf
Lamm n.	lamb
landen	to land
Landkarte f.	map
Landstraße f.	highway
lang	long
langsam	slow
langweilig	boring
Laptop m.	laptop
lassen	to let, allow
Lastwagen m.	truck
laufen	to run
laufende Nase	runny nose
Lebenslauf m.	résumé
Lebensmittelgeschäft n.	grocery store
Lehrer/-in m./f.	teacher
leicht	easy, light
Leid n.	sorrow
leiden	to suffer
Leid tun (sich)	to be sorry
Lenkrad n.	steering wheel
lerneifrig	studious
lesen	to read
lieben	to love
Likör m.	liqueur
Limonade f.	lemonade
Limone f.	lime
links	left
Lippe f.	lip
Liter n.	liter
Loch n.	cavity, hole
Locken drehen	to curl
Löffel m.	spoon
Loge f.	box (theater)
Lohn m.	salary
Lohnerhöhung f.	raise in salary
los	loose, slack
löschen	to delete (computer file)
Luftpost f.	airmail
Luxuswagen m.	luxury car
lyrisch	lyrical
machen	to make, do
Mädchen n.	girl
Magen m.	stomach
Magenschmerzen pl.	stomachache
Mahlzeit f.	meal
Mai m.	May
Mais m.	corn
man	one, someone
Manager m.	manager
Mandel f.	almond
Mann m.	man, husband
Männerkleidung f.	men's clothing
Manschettenknopf m.	cufflink
Mantel m.	coat
Mappe f.	briefcase, folder
Markt m.	market
Marmelade f.	jam, marmelade
März m.	March
Maus f.	mouse
Mechaniker/-in m./f.	mechanic
mechanisch	mechanical
Medikament n.	medication
mehr	more
mein	my
Messer n.	knife
Metzgerei f.	butcher shop
Mexikaner/-in m./f.	Mexican person
mexikanisch	Mexican
Milch f.	milk
Milchladen m.	dairy store
Milchzahn m.	baby tooth
mild	mild

Milliarde f.	billion	*naiv*	naive
Milliliter n.	milliliter	*Name m.*	name
Million f.	million	*Nase f.*	nose
Mindestlohn m.	minimum wage	*national*	national
Mineralwasser n.	mineral water	*Natur f.*	nature
Minirock m.	miniskirt	*neben*	next to
Minute f.	minute	*neblig*	foggy
mit	with	*Neffe m.*	nephew
Mittag m.	noon	*negativ*	negative
Mittagessen n.	lunch	*nein*	no
mittelgroß	medium (size)	*nervös*	nervous
Mitternacht f.	midnight	*neu*	new
Mittwoch m.	Wednesday	*neun*	nine
Mobiltelefon n.	cell phone	*neunzehn*	nineteen
mögen	like, to want to	*neunzig*	ninety
möhre f.	carrot	*nicht*	not
monitor m.	monitor	*Nichte f.*	niece
Montag m.	Monday	*nichts*	nothing
Moped n.	moped	*nie*	never
morgen	tomorrow	*Niederländer/-in m./f.*	Dutch person
Morgen m.	morning	*niedrig*	low
müde	tired	*niemals*	never
Münze f.	coin	*niemand*	no one
müssen	must, to have to	*niesen*	to sneeze
Mund m.	mouth	*noch*	still
Muscheln pl.	mussels	*Norden m.*	north
Museum n.	museum	*Normalbenzin n.*	regular gas
Musik f.	music	*Note f.*	grade; note
Mutter f.	mother	*Notfall m.*	emergency
nach	after; to	*November m.*	November
nach Hause	home (ward)	*Nudeln pl.*	noodles
Nachgebühr f.	postage due	*Nummer f.*	number
Nachname m.	last name	*nur*	only
Nachricht f.	message	*ob*	whether, if
nachschicken	to forward	*oben*	above
nächste	next	*Obst n.*	fruit
Nacht f.	night	*Obstkuchen m.*	pie
Nachtisch m.	dessert	*oder*	or
nah	near	*offen*	open

offensiv	offensive	*Pfeffer m.*	pepper
öffentlich	public	*Pfirsich m.*	peach
öffnen	to open	*Pflaume f.*	plum
ohne	without	*Pförtner m.*	doorman
Ohnmacht f.	faint	*Pfund n.*	pound, 500 grams
Ohr n.	ear	*Pille f.*	pill
Ohrenschmerzen pl.	earache	*Pilot m.*	pilot
Ohrring m.	earring	*Pilz m.*	mushroom
Oktober m.	October	*Platz m.*	seat
Onkel m.	uncle	*Plätzchen n.*	cookie
Oper f.	opera	*Pole/Polin m./f.*	Polish person
Optimist/-in m./f.	optimist	*politisch*	political
Orange f.	orange	*Polizei f.*	police
Orchester n.	orchestra	*Polizeistation f.*	police station
Orgel f.	organ (musical instrument)	*Polizist/-in m./f.*	police officer
örtlich	local	*Pomme frites pl.*	French fries
örtliche betäubung f.	local anesthesia	*populär*	popular
Ortsgespräch n.	local call	*Porto n.*	postage
Osten m.	east	*positiv*	positive
Paket n.	package	*Post f.*	mail, post office
Pampelmuse f.	grapefruit	*Postamt n.*	post office
Panne f.	flat tire, breakdown	*Postanweisung f.*	postal money order
Papier n.	paper	*Posteingang m.*	inbox
Parfüm n.	perfume	*Postkarte f.*	postcard
Park m.	park	*postlagernd*	general delivery
parken	to park	*Postleitzahl f.*	zip code
Parkplatz m.	parking lot	*Präsident/-in m./f.*	president
Party f.	party	*pro*	per
Pass m.	passport	*Problem n.*	problem
Passagier/-in m./f.	passenger	*Professor/-in m./f.*	professor
Passkontrolle f.	passport check	*promovieren*	to earn a doctorate
patriotisch	patriotic	*prost*	cheers
Pendelbus m.	shuttle bus	*Pudding m.*	pudding
Penizillin n.	penicillin	*Pullover m.*	sweater
Pension f.	boarding house	*putzen*	to clean
perfekt	perfect	*Quark m.*	curd cheese, quark
Person f.	person	*Quittung f.*	receipt
Pessimist/-in m./f.	pessimist	*radfahren*	to cycle, ride a bike
Petersilie f.	parsley	*Radiergummi m.*	eraser

rasieren (sich)	to shave
Rathaus n.	city hall
Ratte f.	rat
rauchen	to smoke
reagieren	to react
Rechner m.	calculator
Rechnung f.	bill
rechts	right
Rechtsanwalt/-in m./f.	lawyer
Regen m.	rain
Regenmantel m.	raincoat
Regenschirm m.	umbrella
regnen	to rain
regnerisch	rainy
reinigen	to clean
Reis m.	rice
Reisescheck m.	traveler's check
relativ	relative, relatively
Reparatur f.	repair
reparieren	to repair
Republik f.	republic
Reservierung f.	reservation
Restaurant n.	restaurant
Rezept n.	prescription
Rezeption f.	reception (desk)
R-Gespräch n.	collect call
rhythmisch	rhythmic
Rinderbraten m.	roast beef
Ring m.	ring
Ringmappe f.	binder
Rock m.	skirt
Roggenbrot n.	rye bread
Rollschuh laufen	to rollerskate
romantisch	romantic
rosa	pink
Rose f.	rose
Ross n.	horse, steed
rot	red
Rucksack m.	backpack
rudern	to row
Rücken m.	back
ruhig	calm, quiet
Russe/Russin m./f.	Russian person
Saft m.	juice
sagen	to say
Sahne f.	cream
Sakko m.	sport jacket
Salat m.	salad
Salz n.	salt
Samstag m.	Saturday
Sandalen pl.	sandals
satt	full, satiated
Sauerrahm m.	sour cream
S-Bahn f.	city and suburban train
Scanner m.	scanner
Schach n.	chess
Schachtel f.	box
Schaf n.	sheep
schaffen	to create, get done
Schal m.	scarf, muffler
Schale f.	bowl
Schalter m.	counter, window
Schauspieler m.	actor
Schauspeilerin f.	actress
Scheck m.	check
Scheckbuch n.	checkbook
Scheibenwischer m.	windshield wiper
Scheinwerfer m.	headlight
scherzhaft	joking, playful
Schinken m.	ham
Schlafanzug m.	pajamas
schlafen	to sleep
Schlaflosigkeit f.	insomnia
Schlägerei f.	fist fight
schlampig	sloppy
schlecht	bad
Schlips m.	tie
Schlüpfer m.	panties

Schmuck m.	jewelry	*See m.*	lake
schneiden	to cut	*seekrank*	seasick
schneien	to snow	*Seekrankheit f.*	seasickness
schnell	fast	*segeln*	to sail
Schnellimbiss m.	snackbar	*sehen*	to see
Schokolade f.	chocolate	*sehr*	very
schon	already	*Seife f.*	soap
schön	pretty, nice	*sein*	his, its
schreiben	to write	*sein*	to be
Schreibmaschine f.	typewriter	*Sekretär/-in m./f.*	secretary
Schreibtisch m.	desk	*Sekt m.*	sparkling wine, champagne
Schriftsteller/-in m./f.	writer	*Selterswasser n.*	sparkling water
schüchtern	shy	*senden*	to send
Schuhe pl.	shoes	*Senf m.*	mustard
Schuhgröße f.	shoe size	*September m.*	September
Schularbeit f.	homework	*Service m.*	service
Schulabschluss m.	homework	*Serviette f.*	napkin
Schule f.	school	*setzen (sich)*	to seat oneself
Schüler/-in m./f.	pupil	*Sicherheitskontrolle f.*	security check
Schulter f.	shoulder	*Sie*	you (formal)
Schultertuch n.	shawl	*sie pl.*	they
Schuss m.	shot	*sie sing.*	she, it (feminine)
schwach	weak	*sieben*	seven
schwanger	pregnant	*siebzehn*	seventeen
schwarz	black	*siebzig*	seventy
Schwarzbrot n.	black bread	*siezen*	say *Sie*
Schwede/Schwedin m./f.	Swede person	*Sinfonie f.*	symphony
Schwein n.	pig	*singen*	to sing
Schweinefleisch n.	pork	*Sinusitis f.*	sinusitis
Schweizer/-in m./f.	Swiss person	*Skijacke f.*	ski jacket
schwer	hard, heavy	*Ski laufen*	ski
Schwester f.	sister	*Smoking m.*	tuxedo
Schwimmbad n.	swimming pool	*Snack m.*	snack
schwimmen	to swim	*Socke f.*	sock
schwindlig	dizzy	*Sodbrennen n.*	heartburn
sechs	six	*Sofa n.*	sofa
sechzehn	sixteen	*sofort*	immediately
sechzig	sixty	*Software f.*	software
See f.	sea	*Sohn m.*	son

solid	solid	*Stein m.*	rock, stone
sollen	should	*Stiefel m.*	boot
Sommer m.	summer	*Stil m.*	style
Sommersprossen pl.	freckles	*stimmen*	to be correct
Sonnabend m.	Saturday	*stören*	to disturb
Sonnenbrand m.	sunburn	*Straße f.*	street
Sonnenbrille f.	sunglasses	*Straßenraub m.*	mugging
sonnengebräunt	tan	*strikt*	strict
sonnig	sunny	*Strom m.*	electricity
Sonntag m.	Sunday	*Strumpf m.*	stocking
soviel	as much	*Strumpfhose f.*	pantyhose
sozialistisch	socialistic	*Student/-in m./f.*	student
Spanier/-in m./f.	Spanish person	*Stück n.*	piece
sparen	to save	*stürmisch*	stormy
Spargel m.	asparagus	*Stuhl m.*	chair
Sparkasse f.	savings bank	*Stunde f.*	hour
Sparkonto n.	savings account	*suchen*	to look for, seek
Spaß m.	fun	*Süden m.*	south
spät	late	*Süßigkeiten pl.*	candy
spazieren	to go for a walk	*Süßwarengeschäft n.*	candy store
Speisekarte f.	menu	*Summe f.*	sum, total
Spende f.	donation	*Supermarkt m.*	supermarket
spielen	to play	*Suppe f.*	soup
Spielfilm m.	feature film	*sympathisch*	likeable
Spinat m.	spinach	*synchronisiert*	dubbed
Spinne f.	spider	*System n.*	system
sportlich	athletic	*Tabakwarenhändler m.*	tobacco shop
sprechen	to speak	*Tablett n.*	tray
Spritze f.	injection, shot	*Tablette f.*	tablet, pill
Sprudelwasser n.	carbonated water	*Tag m.*	day
spülen	to wash	*tanken*	to fill up (gas)
Stadt f.	city	*Tankstelle f.*	gas station
Stangenselerie m.	celery	*Tante f.*	aunt
stark	strong	*tanzen*	to dance
Stärke f.	starch	*tapfer*	brave
starten	to take off (aircraft)	*Taschentuch n.*	handkerchief
Statistik f.	statistic	*Tasse f.*	cup
Stau m.	traffic jam	*Tastatur f.*	keyboard
Steak n.	steak	*tausend*	thousand

Taxi n.	taxi	*überqueren*	to cross
Taxistand m.	taxi stand	*Überschwemmung f.*	flood
Tee m.	tea	*Uhr f.*	clock
Telefon n.	telephone	*um*	around
Telefonbuch n.	telephone book	*Umweg m.*	detour
telefonieren	to telephone, call	*umziehen (sich)*	to change clothes
Teller m.	plate	*und*	and
Tennis m.	tennis	*Unfall m.*	accident
teuer	expensive	*ungeduldig*	impatient
Textmarker m.	highlighter	*Unglück n.*	crash, accident
Theater n.	theater	*Universität f.*	university
Tier n.	animal	*unser*	our
Tisch m.	table	*Unsinn m.*	nonsense
Tischerler/-in m./f.	carpenter	*unten*	below
Tochter f.	daughter	*unter*	under
Toilette f.	toilet, restroom	*unterbrochen*	interrupted
Tomate f.	tomato	*Unterhemd n.*	undershirt
Topf m.	pot	*Unterkunft f.*	accomodation
total	total	*Unterrock m.*	slip
tragbar	portable	*unterschreiben*	to sign
tragen	to carry, wear	*Untertasse f.*	saucer
trampen	to hitchhike	*Untertitel m.*	subtitle
Transport m.	transportation	*Unterwäsche f.*	underwear
traurig	sad	*unterwegs*	on the way
Treffen n.	meeting	*Ursache f.*	cause
trinken	to drink	*Vanille f.*	vanilla
Trinkgeld n.	tip, gratuity	*Vase f.*	vase
Tritt m.	kick	*Vater m.*	father
trocknen	to dry	*Vegetarier/-in m./f.*	vegetarian
Trockner m.	dryer	*verbinden*	to connect
Trompete f.	trumpet	*verdienen*	to earn
Truthahn m.	turkey	*vergesslich*	forgetful
tschüss	so long, bye	*Vergewaltigung f.*	rape
T-Shirt n.	t-shirt	*verkaufen*	to sell
Tür f.	door	*Verkehrsampel f.*	traffic light
tun	to do	*Verkehrsstau m.*	traffic jam
Turnschuhe pl.	gym shoes, sneakers	*verlangsamen*	to slow down
U-Bahn f.	subway	*verlegen*	embarrassed
überholen	to pass	*verletzen*	to injure

verleugnen	to deny
verlieren	to lose
verloben (sich)	to get engaged
Verlobte m./f.	fiancé, fiancée
Verlobungsring m.	engagement ring
versichern	to insure
Versicherung f.	insurance
verstehen	to understand
Verstopfung f.	constipation
Vertrag m.	contract
verwirrt	confused
verwunden	to wound
verzeihen	to forgive
Verzeihung f.	forgiveness; excuse me
verzollen	declare
viel	much
viele	many
vier	four
Vierradantrieb m.	four-wheel drive
Viertel n.	quarter
vierzehn	fourteen
vierzig	forty
Visum n.	visa
Vogel m.	bird
Vöglein n.	little bird
Volleyball m.	volleyball
Vollkornbrot n.	whole wheat bread
von	from, of
vor	before, in front of
vorbeifahren	to drive past
vorder	front
Vorführung f.	performance, showing
Vorname m.	first name
Vorsicht f.	caution
Vorspeise f.	appetizer
vorstellen	to introduce
Vorstellung f.	presentation, introduction
Vorstellungsgespräch n.	interview
vorübergehend	temporary

Vorwahl f.	area code
Wagen m.	car
wählen	to dial, choose
Wählton m.	dial tone
während	during
wandern	to hike
Wandtafel f.	blackboard
Wange f.	cheek
wann	when
warm	warm
warum	why
was	what
Wäschedienst m.	laundry service
Wäscherei f.	laundromat
waschen (sich)	to wash oneself
Waschmaschine f.	washing machine
Waschmittel n.	detergent
Wasser n.	water
Wasserski laufen	to water ski
Website f.	website
Wechselkurs m.	exchange rate
wechseln	to exchange
Wechselstube f.	currency exchange
Weckanruf m.	wake-up call
wegen	because of
weh tun	to hurt
Wehen bekommen	to go into labor
Weichspülmittel n.	fabric softener
Wein m.	wine
Weinglas n.	wineglass
Weintraube f.	grape
Weisheitszahn m.	wisdom tooth
weiß	white
weit	far
welcher, welche, welches	which
wenig	little (amount)
weniger	less, fewer
wenn	whenever, if
wer	who

werden	to become, get; shall, will	*Zahnseide f.*	dental floss
Westen m.	west	*Zahnweh n.*	toothache
Wetter n.	weather	*Zeh m.*	toe
wie	how	*zehn*	ten
wieder	again	*zeigen*	to show
wiederholen	to repeat	*Zeit f.*	time
wiegen	to weigh	*Zeitumstellung f.*	jetlag
windig	windy	*Zeitung f.*	newspaper
Windschutzscheibe f.	windshield	*Zeitungskiosk m.*	newspaper stand
Winter m.	winter	*Zelt n.*	tent
wir	we	*Zimmer frei*	bed and breakfast
Wirkung f.	effect	*Zimmer n.*	room
wissen	to know	*Zinssatz m.*	interest rate
wo	where	*Zitrone f.*	lemon
Woche f.	week	*Zoll m.*	customs
wohin	where (to)	*Zoo m.*	zoo
Wohnung f.	apartment	*zu*	to
wollen	to want	*zu Hause*	at home
Wörterbuch n.	dictionary	*Zucker m.*	sugar
Wurst f.	sausage	*Zug m.*	train
Wurzelbehandlung f.	root canal	*Zugang m.*	admittance
zahlen	to pay	*Zugfahrplan m.*	train schedule
zählen	to count	*zurückbleiben*	to stand back
Zahn m.	tooth	*zurückbringen*	to bring back
Zahnarzt m.	dentist (male)	*zurückhaltend*	reserved, guarded
Zahnärztin f.	dentist (female)	*Zusammenstoß m.*	crash
Zahnbürste f.	toothbrush	*zuversichtlich*	confident
Zahnfleisch n.	gums	*zwanzig*	twenty
Zahnfüllung f.	filling	*zwei*	two
Zahnkrone f.	(dental) crown	*Zwiebel f.*	onion
Zahnprothese f.	dentures	*Zwischenlandung f.*	stopover
Zahnreinigung f.	teeth cleaning	*zwölf*	twelve

The gender and number of the nouns listed here is indicated by *m.* for masculine, *f.* for feminine, *n.* for neuter, *sing.* for singular, and *pl.* for plural. Both German and English verbs are provided as infinitives.

a, an	*ein, eine*	anesthesia	*Betäubung f.*
above	*oben*	angry	*böse*
abscess	*Abszess m.*	animal	*Tier n.*
abstract	*abstrakt*	ankle	*Fußgelenk n.*
to accelerate	*beschleunigen*	annoyed	*ärgerlich*
accent	*Akzent m.*	answering machine	*Anrufbeantworter m.*
accident	*Unfall m., Unglück n.*	antibiotic	*Antibiotikum n.*
accommodation	*Unterkunft f.*	apartment	*Wohnung f.*
acquaintance	*Bekannte m./f.*	ape, monkey	*Affe m.*
active	*aktiv*	apparatus, appliance	*Apparat m.*
actor	*Schauspieler m.*	appetite	*Appetit m.*
actress	*Schauspielerin f.*	appetizer	*Vorspeise f.*
address	*Adresse f., Anschrift f.*	apple	*Apfel m.*
admittance	*Zugang m.*	to apply for	*bewerben (sich)*
African person	*Afrikaner/–in m./f.*	apricot	*Aprikose f.*
after	*nach*	April	*April m.*
again	*wieder*	area code	*Vorwahl f.*
against	*gegen*	arm	*Arm m.*
against it	*dagegen*	around	*um*
air conditioning	*Klimaanlage f.*	arrival	*Ankunft f.*
airline company	*Fluggesellschaft f.*	arthritis	*Arthritis f.*
airline passenger	*Fluggast m.*	artichoke	*Artischocke f.*
airline ticket	*Flugticket n.*	artist	*Artist m., Künstler/–in m./f.*
airmail	*Luftpost f.*	as if	*als ob*
airplane	*Flugzeug n.*	as much	*soviel*
airport	*Flughafen m.*	ashamed	*beschämt*
all, everyone	*alle*	to ask	*fragen*
allergic	*allergisch*	asparagus	*Spargel m.*
allergy	*Allergie f.*	aspirin	*Aspirin n.*
almond	*Mandel f.*	asthmatic person	*Asthmatiker/–in m./f.*
alone	*allein*	asthmatic	*asthmatisch*
already	*schon*	at, by	*bei*
also, too	*auch*	at home	*zu Hause*
always	*immer*	athletic	*athletisch, sportlich*
ambulance	*Krankenwagen m.*	ATM	*Geldautomat m.*
America	*Amerika*	attack	*Angriff m.*
American person	*Amerikaner/–in m./f.*	attractive	*attraktiv*
amount	*betrag*	August	*August m.*
and	*und*	aunt	*Tante f.*

automobile	*Auto n., wagen m.*
automatic transmission	*Automatik Getriebe f.*
autumn	*Herbst m.*
away, remote	*entfern f.*
baby	*Baby n.*
baby tooth	*Milchzahn m.*
back	*Rücken m.*
backpack	*Rucksack m.*
bad	*schlecht*
baggage	*Gepäck n.*
baggage check-in counter	*Abfertigungsschalter m.*
baggage claim	*Gepäckausgabe f.*
baker	*Bäcker/-in m./f.*
balcony	*Balkon m.*
ballet	*Ballett n.*
banana	*Banane f.*
bank	*Bank f.*
bank balance	*Kontostand m.*
bank statement	*Kontoauszug m.*
barber, hair stylist	*Friseur/-in m./f.*
barrette	*Haarspange f.*
baseball	*Baseball m.*
basement	*Keller m.*
basketball	*Basketball m., Korbball m.*
bathtub	*Badewanne f.*
Brazilian person	*Brasilianer/-in m./f.*
to be	*sein*
to be afraid	*Angst haben*
to be called	*heißen*
to be correct	*stimmen*
to be glad, happy	*freuen (sich)*
to be sorry	*Leid tun*
bean	*Bohne f.*
bear	*Bär m.*
beautiful, handsome	*hübsch*
because of	*wegen*
because	*denn*

to be acquainted, know	*kennen*
to become, get; shall, will	*werden*
bed	*Bett n.*
bed and breakfast	*Zimmer frei*
beer	*Bier n.*
before, in front of	*vor*
to behave	*benehmen (sich)*
behind	*hinter*
below	*unten*
belt	*Gürtel m.*
beverage	*Getränk n.*
bicycle	*Fahrrad n.*
big, tall	*groß*
bikini	*Bikini m.*
bill	*Rechnung f.*
bill, paper money	*Geldschein m.*
billion	*Milliarde f.*
binder	*Ringmappe f.*
bird	*Vogel m.*
black bread	*Schwarzbrot n.*
black	*schwarz*
blackberry	*Brombeere f.*
blackboard	*Wandtafel f.*
bleach	*Bleichmittel n.*
to bleed	*bluten*
blind	*blind*
blood pressure	*Blutdruck m.*
blouse	*Bluse f.*
to blow dry	*fönen*
blue	*blau*
blueberry	*Blaubeere f., Heidelbeere f.*
boarding card	*Bortkarte, Einsteigekarte f.*
boarding house	*Pension f.*
boat	*Boot n.*
book	*Buch n.*
book of stamps	*Briefmarkenheft n.*
boot	*Stiefel m.*
boring	*langweilig*

boss	Chef/-in m./f.	cake	Kuchen m.
bottle	Flasche f.	calculator	Rechner m.
bow tie; fly	Fliege f.	calf	Kalb n.
bo	Schale f.	to call, phone	anrufen, telefonieren
box (theater)	Loge f.	calm, quiet	ruhig
box	Schachtel f.	can	Dose f.
boxer shorts	Boxershorts pl.	can, to be able to	können
boy	Junge m.	Canadian	Kanadier/-in m./f.
bra	BH m.	candy store	Süßwarengeschäft n.
bracelet	Armband n.	candy	Süßigkeiten pl.
brakelight	Bremslicht n.	canine tooth	Eckzahn m.
brake	Bremse f.	capitalist	Kapitalist/-in m./f.
brassiere	Büstenhalter m.	car	Auto n., Wagen m.
brave	tapfer	carbonated water	Sprudelwasser n.
bread	Brot n.	cards	Karten pl.
break	brechen	carpenter	Tischler/-in m./f.
breakfast	Frühstück n.	carrot	Karotte f., Möhre f.
bride	Braut f.	to carry	tragen
briefcase	Aktentasche f.	to cash (in)	einlösen
briefcase, folder	Mappe f.	cash	bar, Bargeld n.
to bring back	zurückbringen	to catch a cold	erkälten (sich)
broach	Brosche f.	cauliflower	Blumenkohl m.
broken	kaputt	cause	Ursache f.
brother	Bruder m.	caution	Vorsicht f.
brown	braun	cavity, hole	Loch n.
to brush	bürsten	CD-ROM drive	CD-ROM-Laufwerk n.
burglary, break-in	Einbruch m.	celebration	Fest n.
bus	Bus m.	celery	Stangenselerie m.
bus station	Busbahnhof m.	cell phone	Handy n., Mobiltelefon
bus stop	Bushaltestelle f.	CEO	Generaldirektor m.
business card	Geschäftskarte f.	certified	bestätigt
but	aber	chain	Kette f.
but, still	doch	chair	Stuhl m.
butcher shop	Fleischerei f.,	chalk	Kreide f.
	Metzgerei f.	chance	Chance f.
butcher	Fleischer/-in m./f.	change	Änderung f.
butter	Butter f.	change (money)	Kleingeld n.
buttermilk	Buttermilch f.	to change clothes	umziehen (sich)
to buy	kaufen	cheap	billig
by, at	bei	to check in (luggage)	abfertigen, abgeben

check	*Scheck m.*	computer	*Computer m.*
checkbook	*Scheckbuch n.*	conceited	*eingebildet*
check-in desk	*Abfertigungsschalter m.*	concert	*Konzert n.*
checking account	*Girokonto n.*	conference	*Konferenz f.*
cheek	*Backe f., Wange f.*	confident	*zuversichtlich*
cheer	*prost*	confused	*verwirrt*
cheese	*Käse m.*	to connect	*verbinden*
cherry	*Kirsche f.*	constipation	*Verstopfung f.*
chess	*Schach n.*	contract	*Vertrag m.*
chest	*Brust f.*	convertible	*Kabrio n.*
chicken	*Hähnchen n., Huhn n.*	cook, chef	*Koch/Köchin m./f.*
child	*Kind n.*	to cook	*kochen*
chocolate	*Schokolade f.*	cookie	*Plätzchen n.*
to choose	*wählen*	cool	*kühl*
church	*Kirche f.*	copy machine	*Kopiergerät n.*
city	*Stadt f.*	corn	*Mais m.*
city and suburban train	*S-Bahn f.*	correct	*korrekt*
city hall	*Rathaus n.*	corridor	*Korridor m.*
civil servant	*beamter m./beamtin f.*	to cost	*kosten*
class, grade	*Klasse f.*	cough drop	*Hustenbonbon n.*
classroom	*Klassenzimmer n.*	cough syrup	*Hustensaft m.*
to clean	*reinigen*	to count	*zählen*
to clean, polish	*putzen*	counter, window	*Schalter m.*
to click on	*anklicken*	course	*Kursus m.*
clock	*Uhr f.*	cousin	*Cousin m., Cousine f.*
clothing store	*Bekleidungsgeschäft n.*	cow	*Kuh f.*
coat	*Mantel m.*	cowardly	*feige*
cocktail	*Cocktail m.*	cozy, comfortable	*gemütlich*
cocoa	*Kakao m.*	crash, accident	*Unfall m., Unglück n.,*
coffee	*Kaffee m.*		*Zusammenstoß m.*
coin	*Münze f.*	cream	*Sahne f.*
cold (illness)	*Erkältung f.*	cream cheese	*Frischkäse m.*
cold (temperature)	*kalt*	to create, get done	*schaffen*
collect call	*R-Gespräch n.*	credit card	*Kreditkarte f.*
color	*Farbe f.*	critical	*kritisch*
to color, dye	*färben*	to cross	*überqueren*
to come	*kommen*	crown (dental)	*Zahnkrone f.*
communist	*kommunistisch*	cucumber	*Gurke f.*
compact car	*Kompaktwagen m.*	cufflink	*Manschettenknopf m.*
company	*Firma f.*	cummerbund	*Kummerbund m.*

cup	*Tasse f.*	diligent, hard-working	*fleißig*
curd cheese	*Quark m.*	dimple	*Grübchen n.*
to curl	*Locken drehen*	dining room	*Esszimmer n.*
currency exchange	*Geldwechsel m.,*	dinner	*Abendbrot n., Abendessen m.*
	Wechselstube f.	diplomat	*Diplomat m.*
customs	*Zoll m.*	disappointed	*enttäuschat*
to cut	*schneiden*	to disturb	*stören*
cybercafé	*Cybercafé n.*	dizzy	*schwindlig*
to cycle, ride a bike	*radfahren*	to do gardening	*im Garten arbeiten*
dairy store	*Milchladen m.*	to do	*tun*
to dance	*tanzen*	doctor, physician	*Doktorgrad m.*
dark blue	*dunkelblau*	doctorate	*Doktorgrad m.*
daughter	*Tochter f.*	don't mention it	*keine Ursache*
day	*Tag m.*	donation	*Spende f.*
December	*Dezember m.*	door	*Tür f.*
to declare	*verzollen, erklären*	doorman	*Pförtner m.*
decorative pin	*Anstecknadel f.*	double bed	*Doppelbett n.*
to delete (computer file)	*löschen*	doughnut	*Berliner m.*
democratic	*demokratisch*	to download	*herunterladen*
dental floss	*Zahnseide f.*	dress	*Kleid n.*
dentist	*Zahnarzt m.,*	dress size	*Kleidergröße f.*
	Zahnärztin f.	to dress, put on clothes	*anziehen (sich)*
dentures	*Zahnprothese f.*	to drink	*trinkenk*
to deny	*verleugnen*	to drive past	*vorbeifahren*
department academic	*Fakultät f.*	to drive, travel by	*fahrene*
department store	*Kaufhaus n.*	drive, trip	*Fahrt f.*
departure (plane)	*Abflug m.*	driver	*Fahrer m.*
departure	*Abreise f.*	to drown	*ertrinken*
to deposit (money)	*einzahlen*	drugstore	*Drogerie f.*
desk	*Schreibtisch m.*	dry cleaner	*chemische Reinigung f.*
dessert	*Nachtisch m.*	to dry	*trocknen*
detergent	*Waschmittel n.*	dryer	*Trockner m.*
detour	*Umweg m.*	to dye, color	*färben*
diabetic (person)	*Diabetiker/-in m./f.*	dubbed	*synchronisiert*
diabetic	*diabetisch*	during	*während*
dial tone	*Wählton m.*	Dutch person	*Niederländer/-in m./f.*
to dial	*wählen*	each	*jeder, jede, jedes*
diarrhea	*Durchfall m.*	ear	*Ohr n.*
dictionary	*Wörterbuch n.*	earache	*Ohrenschmerzen pl.*
diet	*Diät f.*	early	*früh*

to earn	*verdienen*	examination	*Examen n.*
to earn a doctorate	*promovieren*	exchange rate	*Wechselkurs m.*
earring	*Ohrring m.*	to exchange	*wechseln*
east	*Osten m.*	excited	*aufgeregt*
easy	*leicht*	excuse	*Entschuldigung f.*
to eat	*essen*	excuse me	*Verzeihung f.*
cconomy car	*Economywagen m.*	cxhaustcd	*erschöpft*
effect	*Wirkung f.*	expensive	*teuer*
effective	*effektiv*	to explain, declare	*erklären*
egg	*Ei n.*	explosion	*Explosion f.*
Egyptian person	*Ägypter/-in m./f.*	express delivery	*Eilzustellung f.*
eight	*acht*	express letter	*Eilbrief m.*
eighteeen	*achtzehn*	to extract	*extrahieren*
eighty	*achtzig*	eyeglasses	*Brille f.*
electrician	*Elektriker m.*	eyetooth	*Augenzahn m.*
electricity	*Strom m.*	eye	*Auge n.*
elementary school	*Grundschule*	fabric softener	*weichspülmittel n.*
elephant	*Elefant m.*	face	*Gesicht n.*
elevator	*Fahrstuhl m.*	faint	*Ohnmacht f.*
eleven	*elf*	fair	*fair*
elbow	*Ellbogen m.*	to fall	*fallen*
e-mail	*E-Mail f.*	false, wrong	*falsch*
e-mail address	*E-Mail-Adresse f.*	family	*Familie f.*
embarrassed	*verlegen*	far	*weit*
emergency	*Notfall m.*	farmhand	*Knecht m.*
to employ	*einstellen*	fast	*schnell*
employee	*Angestellte m./f.*	fat	*Fett n.*
enemy	*Feind m.*	fat, thick	*dick*
engagement ring	*Verlobungsring m.*	father	*Vater m.*
engineer	*Ingenieur/-in m./f.*	favor	*Gefallen m.*
England	*England*	fax machine	*Faxgerät n.*
English	*englisch*	feature film	*Spielfilm m.*
Englishman, -woman	*Engländer/-in m./f.*	February	*Februar m.*
enough	*genug*	fee	*Gebühr f.*
envelope	*Briefumschlag m.*	felt	*Filz m.*
equal, same	*gleich*	fever	*Fieber n.*
eraser	*Radiergummi m.*	fewer, less	*weniger*
European person	*Europäer/-in m./f.*	fiancé, fiancée	*Verlobte m./f.*
evening	*Abend m.*	field	*Feld n.*
everyone, everything	*alle, alles*	fifteen	*fünfzehn*

fifty	*fünfzig*	fountain pen	*Füller m.*
file cabinet	*Aktenschrank m.*	four	*vier*
file	*Datei f.*	fourteen	*vierzehn*
to fill up (gas tank)	*tanken*	four-wheel drive	*Vierradantrieb m.*
filling	*Zahnfüllung f.*	freckles	*Sommersprossen pl.*
film, movie	*Film m.*	French fries	*Pomme frites pl.*
final prep school exam	*Abitur n.*	French person	*Franzose/Franzosin m./f.*
to find	*finden*	frequent, frequently	*häufig*
finger	*Finger m.*	fresh	*frisch*
fingernail	*Fingernagel m.*	Friday	*Freitag m.*
fire	*Feuer n.*	friend, boyfriend	*Freund m.*
to fire, release	*entlassen*	friend, girlfriend	*Freundin f.*
firefighter	*Feuerwehrfrau f.,*	friendly	*freundlich*
	Feuerwehrmann m.	frog	*Frosch m.*
first name	*Vorname m.*	from, of	*aus, von*
fish market	*Fischgeschäft n.*	front	*vorder*
fish	*Fisch m.*	frostbite	*Erfrierungen pl.*
to fish	*fischen, angeln*	fruit	*Obst n.*
fist fight	*Schlägerei f.*	full, satiated	*satt*
five	*fünf*	fun	*Spaß m.*
fixed menu	*Gedeck-Karte f.*	funny	*komisch*
to flash lightning	*blitzen*	gain (financial)	*Ertrag m.*
flat tire, breakdown	*Panne f.*	garage	*Garage f.*
flight	*Flug m.*	garden	*Garten m.*
flood	*Überschwemmung f.*	gardening	*Gartenarbeit f.*
flower	*Blume f.*	gardener	*Gärtner/-in m./f.*
flu	*Grippe f.*	gas	*Gas n.*
flute	*Flöte f.*	gas pedal	*Gaspedal n.*
fly	*Fliege f.*	gas station	*Tankstelle f.*
to fly	*fliegen*	gasoline	*Benzin n.*
foggy	*neblig*	gate (airport)	*Flugsteig m.*
foot	*Fuß m.*	general delivery	*postlagernd*
for	*für*	generous	*großzügig*
forgetful	*vergesslich*	German person	*Deutsche m./f.*
to forgive	*verzeihen*	German	*deutsch*
forgiveness; excuse me	*Verzeihung f.*	Germany	*Deutschland*
fork	*Gabel f.*	to get engaged	*verloben (sich)*
forty	*vierzig*	to get, fetch	*holen*
to forward	*nachschicken*	girl	*Mädchen n.*
fountain	*Brunnen m.*	to give up; check in (luggage)	*aufgeben*

to give	*geben*	handbag	*Handtasche f.*
gladly	*gern*	handkerchief	*Taschentuch n.*
glass, jar	*Glas n.*	to hang up (phone)	*aufhängen*
gloves	*Handschuhe pl.*	to happen	*geschehen*
to go (on foot)	*gehen*	happy	*froh*
to go for a walk	*Spazieren*	hard drive	*Festplattenlaufwerk n.*
to go into labor	*Wehen bekommen*	hard	*hart, schwer*
golf	*Golf m.*	hardware (computer)	*Hardware f.*
good, well	*gut*	hat	*Hut m.*
goodbye (on phone)	*auf Wiederhören*	to have	*haben*
goodbye	*auf Wiedersehen*	hayfever	*Heuschnupfen m.*
grade (in school)	*Klasse f.*	he, it (masculine)	*er*
grade, note	*Note n.*	head	*Kopf m.*
gram	*Gramm n.*	headache	*Kopfschmerzen pl.*
granddaughter	*Enkelin f.*	headlight	*Scheinwerfer m.*
grandfather	*Großvater m.*	health	*Gesundheit f.*
grandmother	*Großmutter f.*	healthy	*gesund*
grandson	*Enkel m.*	to hear	*hören*
grape	*Weintraube f.*	heart	*Herz n.*
grapefruit	*Pampelmuse f.*	heartburn	*Sodbrennen n.*
gratuity, tip	*Trinkgeld n.*	to heat	*heizen*
grave	*Grab n.*	heat	*Hitze f.*
gray	*grau*	heavy, hard	*schwer*
green	*grün*	to help	*helfen*
to greet	*grüßen*	help, aid	*Hilfe f.*
grocery store	*Lebensmittelgeschäft n.*	hemorrhoids	*Hämorrhoiden pl.*
groom	*Bräutigam m.*	her	*ihr*
ground floor	*Erdgeschoss n.*	herring	*Hering m.*
guitar	*Gitarre f.*	hi	*hallo*
gums	*Zahnfleisch n.*	high beams	*Fernlicht n.*
gym shoes	*Turnschuhe pl.*	high	*hoch*
hair	*Haar n.*	highchair	*Hochstuhl m.*
hairdo	*Frisur f.*	higher school	*Hochschule f.*
hair stylist	*Friseur/-in m./f.*	high-heel shoes	*hochhackige Schuhe pl.*
half	*halb*	highlighter	*Textmarker m.*
hallway	*Flur, Korridor m.*	highway	*Autobahn, Landstraße f.*
ham	*Schinken m.*	to hike	*wandern*
hand	*Hand f.*	his	*sein*
to hand in	*abgeben*	historic	*historisch*
hand luggage	*Handgepäck n.*	to hitchhike	*trampen*

hockey	*Hockey m.*	to insure	*versichern*
hole, cavity	*Loch n.*	interest rate	*Zinssatz m.*
home(ward)	*nach Hause*	interesting	*interessant*
homework	*Schularbeit f.*	Internet	*Internet n.*
	Hausaufgaben f., Schulabschluss m.	interrupted	*unterbrochen*
honeymoon	*Flitterwochen pl.*	interview	*Vorstellungsgespräch n.*
horse, steed	*Ross n.*	to introduce	*vorstellen*
hospital	*Krankenhaus n.*	introduction; presentation	*Vorstellung f.*
hot	*heiß*	iodine	*Jod n.*
hotel	*Hotel n.*	it	*er (m.), sie (f.), es (n.)*
hour	*Stunde f.*	its	*sein*
house	*Haus n.*	Italian person	*Italiener/-in m./f.*
how	*wie*	Italian	*italienisch*
humid	*feucht*	jacket	*Jacke f.*
hundred	*hundert*	jam	*Marmelade f.*
hunger	*Hunger m.*	January	*Januar m.*
hunt	*Jagd f.*	Japanese person	*Japaner/-in m./f.*
to hunt	*jagen*	Japanese	*japanisch*
to hurt	*weh tun*	jaw	*Kiefer m.*
husband, man	*Mann m.*	jeans	*Jeans pl.*
hyperactive	*aufgedreht*	jetlag	*Zeitumstellung f.*
I	*ich*	jewelry	*Schmuck m.*
ice; ice cream	*Eis n.*	job	*Job m.*
identification	*Ausweis m.*	to jog	*joggen*
if	*ob, wenn*	joking, playful	*scherzhaft*
immediately	*sofort*	juice	*Saft m.*
impatient	*ungeduldig*	July	*Juli m.*
included	*inbegriffen*	June	*Juni m.*
in-box, incoming mail	*Posteingang m.*	keyboard	*Tastatur f.*
Indian (East)	*Inder m.*	kick	*Tritt m.*
industry	*Industrie f.*	kilogram	*Kilo n., Kilogramm n.*
inexpensive	*billig*	kilometer	*Kilometer m.*
infected	*infiziert*	kind	*freundlich*
inhaler	*Inhalationsapparat m.*	kindergarten	*Kindergarten m.*
injection, shot	*Injektion f., Spritze f.*	to kiss	*küssen*
to injure	*verletzen*	kitchen	*Küche f.*
inn	*Gasthof m.*	knee	*Knie n.*
innovative	*innovativ*	knife	*Messer n.*
insomnia	*Schlaflosigkeit f.*	to know	*wissen*
insurance	*Versicherung f.*	to know, be acquainted	*kennen*

lad	*Knabe m.*	lobster	*Hummer m.*
lake	*See m.*	local	*örtlich*
lamb	*Lamm n.*	local anesthesia	*örtliche Betäubung f.*
to land	*landen*	local call	*Ortsgespräch n.*
lane	*Gasse f.*	loneliness	*Einsamkeit f.*
laptop	*Laptop m.*	lonely	*einsam*
last name	*Nachname m.*	long	*lang*
late	*spät*	long-distance call	*Ferngespräch n.*
to laugh	*lachen*	to look at	*ansehen (sich)*
laundry service	*Wäschedienst m.*	to look for, seek	*suchen*
laundromat	*Wäscherei f.*	loose, slack	*los*
lawyer	*Rechtsanwalt/-in m./f.*	to lose	*verlieren*
laxative	*Abführmittel n.*	to love	*lieben*
lazy	*faul*	lover	*Geliebte m./f.*
to lead	*führen*	low	*niedrig*
to leave behind	*hinterlassen*	lunch	*Mittagessen n.*
left	*links*	luxury car	*Luxuswagen m.*
leg	*Bein n.*	lyrical	*lyrisch*
lemon	*Zitrone f.*	mail; post office	*Post f.*
lemonade	*Limonade f.*	mailbox	*Briefkasten m.*
less, fewer	*weniger*	main course	*Hauptgericht n.*
to let, allow	*lassen*	major subject	*Hauptfach n.*
letter	*Brief m.*	to make, do	*machen*
lettuce	*Kopfsalat m.*	man, husband	*Mann m.*
to lie down	*hinlegen (sich)*	manager	*Manager m.*
light blue	*hellblau*	many	*viele*
light, easy	*leicht*	map	*Landkarte f.*
to like	*gern haben*	March	*März m.*
to like, want to	*mögen*	market	*Markt m.*
likeable	*sympatisch*	marmelade, jam	*Marmelade f.*
lime	*Limone f.*	to marry	*heiraten*
to limp	*hinken*	to matriculate	*immatrikulieren*
lip	*Lippe f.*	May	*Mai m.*
liqueur	*Likör m.*	may, to be allowed	*dürfen*
liter	*Liter n.*	meal	*Mahlzeit f.*
little (amount)	*wenig*	to mean	*bedeuten*
little bird	*Vöglein n.*	mean, nasty	*gemein*
little bit	*bisschen*	meat	*Fleisch n.*
loaf	*Laib m.*	mechanic	*Mechaniker/-in m./f.*
loan	*Darlehen n.*	mechanical	*mechanisch*

medication	*Medikament n.*	mustard	*Senf m.*
medium (size)	*mittelgroß*	my	*mein*
medium well/rare	*halb durchgebraten*	naive	*naiv*
to meet	*kennen lernen*	name	*Name m.*
meeting	*Treffen n.*	napkin	*Serviette f.*
men's clothing	*Männerkleidung f.*	national	*national*
menu	*Speisekarte f.*	nature	*Natur f.*
message	*Nachricht f.*	near	*nah*
Mexican person	*Mexikaner/-in m./f.*	neck	*Hals m.*
Mexican	*mexikanisch*	neckscarf	*Halstuch n.*
midnight	*Mitternacht f.*	necklace	*Halskette f.*
mild	*mild*	to need	*brauchen*
milk	*Milch f.*	negative	*negativ*
milliliter	*Milliliter n.*	nephew	*Neffe m.*
million	*Million f.*	nervous	*nervös*
mineral water	*Mineralwasser n.*	Netherlander	*Niederländer/-in m./f.*
minimum wage	*Mindestlohn m.*	new	*neu*
miniskirt	*Minirock m.*	never	*nie, niemals*
minute	*Minute f.*	newspaper stand	*Zeitungskiosk m.*
mittens	*Fausthandschuhe pl.*	newspaper	*Zeitung f.*
molar	*Backenzahn m.*	next to	*neben*
Monday	*Montag m.*	next	*nächste*
money	*Geld n.*	niece	*Nichte f.*
monitor	*Monitor, Bildschirm m.*	night	*Nacht f.*
moped	*Moped n.*	nine	*neun*
more	*mehr*	nineteen	*neunzehn*
morning	*Morgen m.*	ninety	*neunzig*
mother	*Mutter f.*	no	*nein*
mouse	*Maus f.*	no, not one	*kein*
mouth	*Mund m.*	no one	*niemand*
movie theater	*Kino n.*	no vacancy	*belegt*
Mr., sir	*Herr m.*	nonsense	*Unsinn m.*
much	*viel*	noodles	*Nudeln pl.*
mugging	*Straßenraub m.*	noon	*Mittag m.*
museum	*Museum n.*	north	*Norden m.*
mushroom	*Pilz m.*	nose	*Nase f.*
music	*Musik f.*	not	*nicht*
mussels	*Muscheln pl.*	note; grade	*Note f.*
must, to have to	*müssen*	notebook	*Heft n.*

nothing	*nichts*	paper	*Papier n.*
November	*November m.*	paper clip	*Büroklammer f.*
number	*Nummer f.*	to park	*parken*
nurse	*Krankenschwester f.*	park	*Park m.*
occupation	*Beruf m.*	parking lot	*Parkplatz m.*
occupied	*besetzt*	parsley	*Petersilie f.*
October	*Oktober m.*	party	*Party f.*
of	*von*	to pass	*überholen*
offensive	*offensiv*	passenger	*Passagier m.*
old	*alt*	passport check	*Passkontrolle f.*
on the way	*unterwegs*	passport	*Pass m.*
on	*auf*	pastry shop	*Konditorei f.*
once	*einmal*	patient	*geduldig*
one another, each other	*einander*	patriotic	*patriotisch*
one	*eins*	to pay, pay for	*bezahlen, zahlen*
one, someone	*man*	peace	*Frieden m.*
one-way street	*Einbahnstraße f.*	peach	*Pfirsich m.*
onion	*Zwiebel f.*	peanut	*Erdnuss f.*
only	*nur*	pear	*Birne f.*
open (adjective)	*offen*	peas	*Erbsen pl.*
to open	*öffnen, aufmachen*	pen (fountain)	*Füller m.*
open-minded	*aufgeschlossen*	pencil	*Bleistift m.*
opera	*Oper f.*	pendant	*Anhänger m.*
optimist	*Optimist/-in m./f.*	penicillin	*Penizillin n.*
or	*oder*	pepper	*Pfeffer m.*
orange (fruit)	*Apfelsine f.*	per	*pro*
orange (color or fruit)	*Orange f.*	perfect	*perfekt*
orchestra	*Orchester n.*	performance, showing	*Aufführung f.*
to order	*bestellen*		*Vorstellung f.*
organ (musical instrument)	*Orgel f.*	perfume	*Parfüm n.*
our	*unser*	permanent wave	*Dauerwelle f.*
out, from	*aus*	person	*Person f.*
outgoing	*kontaktfreudig*	pessimist	*Pessimist/-in m./f.*
over there	*dort drüben*	pet	*Haustier n.*
package	*Paket n.*	pharmacist	*Apotheker/-in m./f.*
pajamas	*Schlafanzug m.*	pharmacy, drugstore	*Apotheke f.*
panties	*Schlüpfer m.*	photo	*Foto n.*
pants	*Hose f.*	physician, doctor	*Arzt/Ärztin m./f.*
pantyhose	*Strumpfhose f.*	piano	*Klavier n.*

picture postcard	*Ansichtskarte f.*	pretty, nice	*schön*
pie	*Obstkuchen m.*	print, printing	*Druck m.*
piece	*Stück n.*	printer	*Drucker m.*
pig	*Schwein n.*	problem	*Problem n.*
pill	*Pille f.*	professor	*Professor/-in m./f.*
pillow	*Kissen n.*	to prove	*beweisen*
pilot	*Pilot m.*	public	*öffentlich*
pink	*rosa*	pudding	*Pudding m.*
plate	*Teller m.*	pupil	*Schüler/-in m./f.*
to play	*spielen*	quark, curd cheese	*Quark m.*
please	*bitte*	quarter	*Viertel n.*
plum	*Pflaume f.*	quiet, calm	*ruhig*
plumber	*Klampner/-in m./f.*	to rain	*regnen*
Polish person	*Pole/Polin m./f.*	rain	*Regen m.*
police officer	*Polizist/-in m./f.*	raincoat	*Regenmantel m.*
police station	*Polizeistation f.*	rainy	*regnerisch*
police	*Polizei f.*	raise in salary	*Lohnerhöhung f.*
political	*politisch*	rape	*Vergewaltigung f.*
popular	*populär*	rare (meat)	*englisch gebraten*
pork	*Schweinefleisch n.*	raspberry	*Himbeere f.*
portable	*tragbar*	rat	*Ratte f.*
positive	*positiv*	to react	*reagieren*
post office	*Post f., Postamt n.*	to read	*lesen*
postage	*Porto n.*	receipt	*Quittung f.*
postage due	*Nachgebühr f.*	to receive	*empfangen*
postal money order	*Postanweisung f.*	receiver (telephone)	*Hörer m.*
postcard	*Postkarte f.*	receiver, addressee	*Empfänger/-in m./f.*
pot	*Topf m.*	reception (desk)	*Rezeption f.*
potato	*Kartoffel f.*	receptionist (hotel)	*Empfangschef m.,*
poultry	*Geflügel n.*		*Empfangsdame f.*
pound	*Pfund n.*	red	*rot*
to pour	*gießen*	registered	*eingeschrieben*
pregnant	*schwanger*	regular gas	*Normalbenzin n.*
prep school	*Gymnasium n.*	relative, relatively	*relativ*
prep school diploma	*Arbitur n.*	to release, fire	*entlassen*
prescription	*Rezept n.*	remedy	*Heilmittel n.*
present, gift	*Geschenk n.*	remote, away	*entfernt*
presentation	*Vorführung, Vorstellung f.*	to repair	*reparieren*
president	*Präsident m.*	repair	*Reparatur f.*

to repeat	*wiederholen*	to save	*sparen*
to replace	*ersetzen*	savings account	*Sparkonto n.*
republic	*Republik f.*	savings bank	*Sparkasse f.*
reservation	*Reservierung f.*	to say *du*	*duzen*
reserved, guarded	*Zurückhaltend*	to say *Sie*	*siezen*
restaurant	*Restaurant n.*	to say	*sagen*
résumé	*Lebenslauf m.*	scanner	*Scanner m.*
rhythmic	*rhythmisch*	scarf, muffler	*Schal m.*
ribbon	*Band n.*	school	*Schule f.*
rice	*Reis m.*	screen, monitor	*Bildschirm m.*
to ride a bike	*radfahren*	sea	*See f.*
right	*rechts*	seasick	*seekrank*
to ring	*klingeln*	seasickness	*Seekrankheit f.*
ring	*Ring m.*	to seat oneself	*setzen (sich)*
to rinse	*durchspülen*	seat	*Platz m.*
rinse out	*ausspülen*	secretary	*Sekretär/-in m./f.*
roast beef	*Rinderbraten m.*	security check	*Sicherheitskontrolle f.*
roll	*Brötchen n.*	to see	*sehen*
rollerskate	*Rollschuh laufen*	to sell	*verkaufen*
romantic	*romantisch*	to send	*senden*
room	*Zimmer n.*	sender	*Absender m.*
root canal	*Wurzelbehandlung f.*	September	*September m.*
rose	*Rose f.*	serious	*ernst*
round-trip airline ticket		servant (girl)	*Dienstmädchen n.*
	Hin-und-Rückflugkarte f.	service; call to the waiter	*Bedienung f.*
to row	*rudern*	service	*Service m.*
to run	*laufen*	seven	*sieben*
runny nose	*laufende Nase*	seventeen	*siebzehn*
Russian person	*Russe/Russin m./f.*	seventy	*siebzig*
rye bread	*Roggenbrot n.*	to shave	*rasieren (sich)*
sad	*traurig*	shawl	*Schultertuch n.*
to sail	*segeln*	she, it (feminine)	*sie sing.*
salad	*Salat m.*	sheep	*Schaf n.*
salary	*Lohn m.*	shirt	*Hemd n.*
salt	*Salz n.*	shoe size	*Schuhgröße f.*
same, equal	*gleich*	shoes	*Schuhe pl.*
Saturday	*Samstag, Sonnabend m.*	to shop	*einkaufen*
saucer	*Untertasse f.*	shop	*Laden m.*
sausage	*Wurst f.*	shopping center	*Einkaufszentrum n.*

short	*kurz*	sofa	*Sofa n.*
shot	*Schuss m.*	software	*Software f.*
shot, injection	*Spritze f.*	solid	*solid*
should	*sollen*	someone	*jemand*
shoulder	*Schulter f.*	something	*etwas*
to show	*zeigen*	son	*Sohn m.*
shower	*Dusche f.*	sophisticated	*kultiviert*
shuttle bus	*Pendelbus m.*	sorrow	*Leid n.*
shy	*schüchtern*	soup	*Suppe f.*
sick	*krank*	sour cream	*Sauerrahm m.*
to sign	*unterschreiben*	south	*Süden m.*
to sing	*singen*	Spanish person	*Spanier/-in m./f.*
sinusitis	*Sinusitis f.*	sparkling water	*Selterswasser n.*
sister	*Schwester f.*	sparkling wine, champagne	*Sekt m.*
to sit down	*hinsetzen (sich)*	to speak	*sprechen*
six	*sechs*	speed limit	*Geschwindikeits-*
sixteen	*sechzehn*		*beschränkung f.*
sixty	*sechzig*	to spend (money)	*ausgeben*
size	*Größe f.*	spider	*Spinne f.*
to ski	*Ski laufen*	spinach	*Spinat m.*
ski jacket	*Skijacke f.*	spoon	*Löffel m.*
skirt	*Rock m.*	sport jacket	*Sakko m.*
to sleep	*schlafen*	spouse	*Gatte m., Gattin f.*
slip	*Unterrock m.*	spring	*Frühling m.*
sloppy	*schlampig*	stamp	*Briefmarke f.*
to slow down	*verlangsamen*	to stand back	*zurückbleiben*
slow	*langsam*	staple	*Heftklammer f.*
small, little	*klein*	stapler	*Hefter m.*
smart, clever	*klug*	starch	*Stärke f.*
to smoke	*rauchen*	statistic	*Statistik f.*
snack	*Snack m.*	to stay, remain	*bleiben*
snackbar	*Schnellimbiss m.*	steak	*Steak n.*
sneakers	*Turnschutie pl.*	steering wheel	*Lenkrad n.*
to snow	*schneien*	still	*noch*
so long, bye	*tschüss*	still, but	*doch*
soap	*Seife f.*	stocking	*Strumpf m.*
soccer	*Fußball m.*	stomach	*Magen m.*
socialistic	*sozialistisch*	stomachache	*Magenschmerzen pl.*
sock	*Socke f.*	stone, rock	*Stein m.*

to stop, cease	*aufhören*	system	*System n.*
stopover	*Zwischenlandung f.*	table	*Tisch m.*
store	*Geschäft n.*	tablet, pill	*Tablette f.*
storm	*Gewitter n.*	to take a shower	*duschen (sich)*
stormy	*stürmisch*	to take off (aircraft)	*starten*
straight ahead	*geradeaus*	to take off, take from	*abnehmen*
stranger	*Fremde m./f.*	tall, big	*groß*
strawberry	*Erdbeere f.*	tan	*sonnengebräunt*
street	*Straße f.*	taxi	*Taxi n.*
strict	*strikt*	taxi stand	*Taxistand m.*
to stroll	*bummeln*	tea	*Tee m.*
strong	*stark*	teacher	*Lehrer m.*
student	*Student/-in m./f.*	teeth cleaning	*Zahnreinigung f.*
studious	*lerneifrig*	telephone	*Telefon n.*
stupid	*dumm*	telephone book	*Telefonbuch n.*
style	*Stil m.*	television program	*Fernsehsendung f.*
subject	*Fach n.*	television set	*Fernsehapparat m.*
subtitle	*Untertitel m.*	temporary	*vorübergehend*
subway	*U-Bahn f.*	ten	*zehn*
to suffer	*leiden*	tennis	*Tennis m.*
sugar	*Zucker m.*	tent	*Zelt n.*
suit	*Anzug m.*	to thank	*danken*
sum, total	*Summe f.*	that (conjunction)	*dass*
summer	*Sommer m.*	that	*jener, jene, jenes*
sunburn	*Sonnenbrand m.*	the (feminine)	*die*
Sunday	*Sonntag m.*	the (masculine)	*der*
sunglasses	*Sonnenbrille f.*	the (neuter), that	*das*
sunny	*sonnig*	theater	*Theater n.*
super highway	*Autobahn f.*	theft	*Diebstahl m.*
supermarket	*Supermarkt m.*	their	*ihr*
supper	*Abendbrot n., Abendessen n.*	there is/are	*es gibt*
surname	*Familienname m.*	there	*da, dort*
sweater	*Pullover m.*	they	*sie pl.*
Swedish person	*Schwede/Schwedin m./f.*	thief	*Dieb m.*
to swim	*schwimmen*	thin	*dünn*
swimming pool	*Schwimmbad n.*	thirst	*Durst m.*
swimsuit	*badeanzug m.*	thirteen	*dreizehn*
Swiss person	*Schweizer/-in m./f.*	thirty	*dreißig*
symphony	*Sinfonie f.*	this	*dieser, diese, dieses*

thousand	*tausend*	t-shirt	*T-Shirt n.*
three	*drei*	Tuesday	*Dienstag m.*
through	*durch*	turkey	*Truthahn m.*
to throw up	*erbrechen (sich)*	to turn	*einbiegen*
thumb	*Daumen m.*	to turn off	*abschalten*
to thunder	*donnern*	to turn on	*anschalten*
Thursday	*Donnerstag m.*	turn signal	*Blinker m.*
tie clasp	*Krawattenhalter m.*	tuxedo	*Smoking m.*
tie	*Schlips m.*	twelve	*zwölf*
time	*Zeit f.*	twenty	*zwanzig*
tin	*Büchse f.*	two	*zwei*
tip, gratuity	*Trinkgeld n.*	typewriter	*Schreibmaschine f.*
tired	*müde*	ugly	*hässlich*
to	*nach, zu*	umbrella	*Regenschirm m.*
tobacco shop	*Tabakwarenhändler m.*	uncle	*Onkel m.*
today	*heute*	under	*unter*
toe	*Zeh m.*	undershirt	*Unterhemd n.*
toilet, restroom	*Toilette f.*	to understand	*verstehen*
tomato	*Tomate f.*	underwear	*Unterwäsche f.*
tomorrow	*morgen*	to undress, take off clothes	*ausziehen*
tooth	*Zahn m.*		*(sich)*
toothache	*Zahnweh n.*	unemployed	*arbeitslos*
toothbrush	*Zahnbürste f.*	university	*Universität f.*
total amount	*Betrag m.*	until	*bis*
total	*total*	vanilla	*Vanille f.*
towel	*Handtuch n.*	vase	*Vase f.*
traffic jam	*Verkehrsstau m., Stau*	veal	*Kalbfleisch n.*
traffic light	*Verkehrsampel f.*	vegetarian	*Vegetarier/-in m./f.*
train	*Zug m.*	very	*sehr*
train platform	*Bahnsteig m.*	violin	*Geige f.*
train schedule	*Zugfahrplan m.*	visa	*Visum n.*
train station	*Bahnhof m.*	to visit	*besuchen*
transportation	*Transport m.*	volleyball	*Volleyball m.*
traveler's check	*Reisescheck m.*	waiter, server	*Kellner/-in m./f.*
tray	*Tablett n.*	wake-up call	*Weckanruf m.*
trillion	*Billion f.*	wallet	*Brieftasche f.*
trip, drive	*Fahrt f.*	to want	*wollen*
truck	*Lastwagen m.*	wardrobe	*Kleiderschrank m.*
trumpet	*Trompete f.*	warm	*warm*

to wash oneself	*waschen (sich)*	wine glass	*Weinglas n.*
to wash	*spülen*	winter	*Winter m.*
washing machine	*Waschmaschine f.*	wisdom tooth	*Weisheitszahn m.*
to watch televeision	*fernsehen*	with	*mit*
to water ski	*Wasserski laufen*	withdraw money	*abheben*
water	*Wasser n.*	without	*ohne*
we	*wir*	woman	*Frau f.*
weak	*schwach*	women's clothing	*Frauenkleidung f.*
to wear	*tragen*	work, job	*Arbeit f.*
weather	*Wetter n.*	worried	*besorgt*
website	*Website f.*	to wound	*verwunden*
wedding anniversary	*Hochzeitstag m.*	wrinkles	*Falten pl.*
wedding ring	*Ehering m.*	wrist	*Handgelenk n.*
wedding	*Hochzeit f.*	to write	*schreiben*
Wednesday	*Mittwoch m.*	writer	*Schriftsteller/-in m./f.*
week	*Woche f.*	wrong, false	*falsch*
to weigh	*wiegen*	yellow	*gelb*
weight	*Gewicht n.*	yes	*ja*
well, fountain	*Brunnen m.*	yogurt	*Joghurt m.*
well	*gut*	you (formal)	*Sie*
well-done (meat)	*durchgebraten*	you (plural, informal)	*ihr*
west	*Westen m.*	you (singular, informal)	*du*
what	*was*	your (du)	*dein*
when	*wann*	your (ihr)	*euer*
whenever, if	*wenn*	your (Sie)	*Ihr*
where (to)	*wohin*	zip code	*Postleitzahl f.*
where	*wo*	zoo	*Zoo m.*
whether, if	*ob*		
which	*welcher, welche, welches*		
white	*weiß*		
who	*wer*		
whole wheat bread	*Vollkornbrot n.*		
why	*warum*		
wife, woman	*Frau f.*		
window	*Fenster n.*		
windshield wiper	*Scheibenwischer m.*		
windshield	*Windschutzscheibe f.*		
windy	*windig*		
wine	*Wein m.*		

Index